Expressions of Poetry in Season

by

Katherine Hagans Clark

All Rights Reserved
Copyright © 2014 by Katherine Hagans Clark

No part of this book may be reproduced or transmitted, downloaded, distributed, reverse engineered, or stored in or introduced into any information storage and retrieval system, in any form or by any means, including photocopying and recording, whether electronic or mechanical, now known or hereinafter invented without permission in writing from the publisher.

Dorrance Publishing Co
701 Smithfield Street
Pittsburgh, PA 15222
Visit our website at *www.dorrancebookstore.com*

ISBN: 978-1-4349-3711-7
eISBN: 978-1-4349-3631-8

Expressions of Poetry in Season

Contents

About the Author and the Book

This introduction gives a necessarily extensive view of myself as the author of a *first book*...My mother was born in 1909 to parents who were descendants of slaves – linage dating back to the 1600s, from Africans uprooted from their native lands and transplanted as the American slaves... My father, was born in 1901. His father, born in the 1800s, was a descendant of slaves. His mother, a Cherokee Indian, was born in 1875. Her parents were the offspring of Cherokee ancestry, who were among the approximately one thousand of Indians who in the early 1800s, escaped the *Trail of Tears Massacre* and hid in the hills of western North Carolina. Afterwards, they migrated eastward to safety, settling in territories (located in present day Wayne County North Carolina) I am a seventy five years old American, with African and Cherokee Indian ancestry.

I begun writing poetry in my early thirties. "*Expressions of Poetry in Season*" is a celebration of memories, romance, love, motivations, spirituality, and harmony, and ends with a special *Noteworthy Living Experience.*

The other day an acquaintance said to me, " Aren't you to old to be publishing your *first book?*

My passion to write, is not based solely on my age as a number... but also upon my character growth, applying to experiences and life lessons. In this technological world of information, I also have a voice...so does my motto, *Recognize the sunflowers abiding amidst the weeds.*

During a period in 1971, I was undergoing a repentant frame of mind; needing the Lord and Savior Jesus Christ for direction. Finally, placing the utmost faith in Him, I submitted my sins into the hands of His mercy. He answered my plea with the blessing of redemption. I evolved to know the Son of God, as *The Power to Forgive* – to judge my heart and soul, the motives behind my experiences good or bad, the complications, mistakes and short comings; as well as adversity surely at times to occur. He abides over the roots of destiny I have no control over. Having been blessed with a new relationship with the Lord, I evolved as a person who seeks *His Alternative Wisdom* for spiritual growth.

Minnie Jean Hagans is the name I was given at birth. I can't even remember when my dad first nicknamed me "Cat," probably as a toddler;

from then on my family members called me only by my nick name. My dad at times laughed at my behavior patterns as "cat – like," as in affectionate but could become quite temperamental. (Much later in life, having developed self – awareness as a woman, yet questioning my upbringing as a child...I was never a person, even as a child, who would deliberately offend anyone...so why did I have to be so temperamental?...The answer became apparent, I was much too often provoked by certain female family members, as though it was a normal thing to do; I grew up having to consume their negative energy. As a woman, I realized that even within a close knit family, such as mines, it is common that dysfunctional habits are practiced, but by a rather psychological lack of understanding or communication; the problem is that favoritism can be passed on as generational.)

After finishing high school, I moved to Brooklyn, NY. My name change was rather creative; I identified with my nickname (but chose to spell it with a K) Kat became short for Katherine, I dropped Minnie Jean altogether.

I grew up in the 1940s in Wilson County, NC. My dad was a farmer, under the sharecropping system that demanded the help of his older children. However, the younger ones at around eight years old had to help out as well; actually child laborers, as well as other young children across the South, working under the supervision of the older family members. I was the sixth child of one brother and four sisters (years later there would be an additional two girls and one more boy). The sharecropping system did a pitiful job at sharing the profits. The owner's profits we produced kept him rich ~ we remained poor. Sharecroppers across the South contributed to the rising economy during the post- Depression era, especially by the major cash crop of cotton and tobacco.

Revealing more in depth what led to my spiritual experience back in 1971, I was undergoing a soul searching crisis, on the verge of a nervous breakdown – at a breaking point from feeling overwhelming distress, especially about my four children being caught in between the conflicting relationship of their two parents. I had no way out it seemed. This situation could not help but have an unhealthy impact on the lives of the children as well as myself. By the grace of God, I find the courage to take my children with me, from Brooklyn to Charlotte NC, leaving behind their excessively drinking father. He would eventually stop drinking, but excessive as well was the damage it caused to his health.

I, at the age of thirty seven years old, had for one year taken on the responsibility as the sole supporter of my children, Kim, age fifteen, Karen, age eleven, Jaki, age nine and Stanley Jr., age seven. In Charlotte we lived in a community that bared quite a bit of the negative side of life. We (except Kim) became members of a small family oriented Baptist Church named Chappell Memorial. Most of the members, old and young took active roles in various ministries under leadership promoting *team-play.* I was inspired by that sincere display of togetherness and, before long, I with the children, became active members also. The Church served as a social outlet for us as well as a spiritual support system.

Working at Iveys, one of Charlotte's most upscale Department stores, (at the time), doing alterations on garments for customers, gave me the opportunity to accomplish sewing skills on a professional level. Out of the need to earn some supplementary income, I organized an in- home sewing business, making garments, plus doing alterations for personal clients. By no means becoming wealthy but becoming a *realist*, by carrying the weight of circumstances seeming too harsh to convey – some cases I could not change, required staying focused by my relationship with Jesus Christ, in order to remain a devoted *single parent.*

The children became young adults and moved on in their lives, but the support system between us remained intact, including our traditional *get together*. Life gives… life takes away, was the part extremely hard to accept by the death of my son Junior at the young age of twenty six. The grief over my son's death took its toll on me before subsiding… I finally gained the strength to appreciate having shared with his beloved life on earth…

"Change begins at the bottom!" said Senator, Barack Obama, in the 2008 Presidential campaign … I thought *back in the day* – the small church making a humble stand on Christian principles… I thought about a period during the children's early adulthood when confusion and unrest entered in between us – *differences colliding*. I prayed for something much more powerful to remain even through the differences and that is the *team-play* we exercised in a community at the bottom of the social scale. We upheld boundaries up against the opposition – *we had each other's back*. Even though Kim did her own thing – *"now you see her, now you don't"*, our love for her remained stable, included always in our daily prayers.

Dedication

Expressions of Poetry in Season, is dedicated to my offspring, present and future.

Acknowledgment

Expressions of Poetry in Season, a creative categorization of sentiments, from my innermost feelings, gives my overall conception that it takes cultivation for the exalting of the human spirit. In "A Noteworthy Living Experience," I recognize important historical events, historical concepts, and legendary figures.

As a young lady, I eye-witnessed certain events of the very tumultuous 1950s and 60s Civil Rights Movement, dramatized very often, on national television, from its beginning to its ending. The non-violent struggles of crusaders for a more just society; massive blood-shed, loss of lives, finally proved to be effective, for the proposal of the Civil Rights Act to become the law of the land in 1964.

I was born into a society that had already shaped my existence as the inferior child of society. The Movement made me an heir to the exaltation of my *Americanism in the land of the free*. The Movement is dear to my heart forever.

Millions of American citizens struggled through the transformational growing pains, evolving with a better "fellow American" race relationship, rising about the racial bigotry. But flaws dismissed –or not known about, are apt to be repeated.

My poem about Frederick Douglass was created through studying about his life as a slave, from the book, written by himself: *Narratives of the Life of Frederick Douglass, an American Slave*: Boston: published at the Anti-slavery office. No. 25 Cornwell; copyright 1845. Douglass was a pioneer for the abolishing of slavery, as well for the civil rights of former slaves. Frederick Douglass powerful work for the civil rights of humanity, still today lives in the hearts of individuals concerned for their fellowman.

Perilous events were constantly playing out on the evening news, surrounding the presidency of John F. Kennedy. On June 11, 1963, I observed him delivering an Address to the nation. A great many years later, I had a need to write an excerpt from Kennedy's Address for my book, *Expressions of Poetry in Season*. Especially to write the Address in its original wording, I turned to the book, I had purchased in 1965, a couple of years following the death of Kennedy: *John Fitzgerald Kennedy; as we remember him*. Author: Joan

Simpson Burns; Goddard Lieberson; Ira Teichberg. Publisher: New York Atheneum, 1965. Kennedy's Address was delivered to the nation; I took it personal, as a keepsake, for Kennedy cared about lifting me from the *inferior child, in the land of the free!* Kennedy called out bigotry for what it was!

Martin Luther King Jr., his challenges for the civil rights for his American sisters and brothers, almost seemed effortless, yet he was plagued by the dangerous task. Excerpts from Martin's *I Have a Dream Speech*, I wrote in its originality from the book, *My Life with Martin Luther King Jr.*, by Coretta Scott King; copyright 1969.

Robert Kennedy, as I watched his campaign unfold – having become the leading candidate for the presidential Nomination, Kennedy stole my heart. I felt he would be the president to bridge the racial gap in America!

Coretta Scott King, her always poised presence, on television, was inspirational to watch, under an unimaginable magnitude of stress. I captured her grace in a poem. Also an excerpt from her book: *My Life with Martin Luther King Jr.*

Yesterday's work, by today's martyrs, reminds us Americans of the races, where we came from – as to determine which path we want to follow-going backwards or moving forward? Is the question.

Reminiscing

1940's, I'm nine years, in center front as "The Good Fairy" in a play with fourth grade classmates.

Calmness of the Raindrops

Provocative attitudes surrounds, on a day I wouldn't forget
meditating on keeping at peace, the outrage, was exhausting
through discerning the mysterious presence of Jesus Christ
He understood, I would be ready to meet Him, in the evening
Looking back on the day of my Redemption…I surrendered
my sins in the hands Of Jesus Christ on that wonderful day
still a part of me was missing…I needed to find the child
I left behind… and the search begun with writing about her
The midwife's hands grasped onto the new baby girl
born during The Depression, to parents out of work as farmers
with five children and the baby was another mouth to feed
the little girl, grew up with a natural need for *self-expression*
She grew temperamental, by not enough affectionate attention
the child, misunderstood, was being labeled "mean and wild"
I found the child, and understood, she is who I am: creative
by a sense of imagination, intellectually inclined, a strong willed
individualist, now with *self-awareness no longer suppressed*

Vivid Images

At the two story unpainted house, along a busy road
pigeons flock on top of the shingle roof
a pecan tree provides the front yard with shade
a red rose bush is at one side of the house
on the other side, a garden of vegetables and flowers
collard greens, string beans, tomatoes, cucumbers
geraniums, petunias, pansies and daises
a water pump is on the back porch
three tin tubs rest on empty wooden barrels
one tub for washing cloths the other two for rinsings
cloths are prewashed by hand on a scrub board
then boiled in the backyard wrought iron wash pot
afterwards the wash load gets the final rinsing
the clothsline holds the weekly wash on target
Tricksy's backyard doghouse goes virtually unoccupied
Tom Cat, flees, inside the front door
safe from the growling and barking of Tricksy
Tricksy has nothing more to do, but to dig up the daises
Outer facilities include a toolshed, a cowshed
a mule stable, a pigsty, smokehouse, the toilet
The farmland in constant tillage, is fertile for vegetation
surrounded by woodland herbs and shrubbery
amid hills of earthly gritless clay dirt, pleasing to eat
wild flowers, dandelions, dogwood trees, pine trees
the fishing pond, the apple tree, the Spring of Water
A special time and place shaping the origin of my youth
there were chores to go around, more than enough
a place of unforgettable images, is where I grew up

Abiding Above the Struggle

Folk are adding the laughter and sharing in the sorrow
It's the 1940s Post- Depression era
neighbors far and near lend a helping hand
the schoolhouse is entwining with the family structure
the churchhouse is adding song and dance for living
instilling faith abiding above the struggle
the congregation is worshipping the *Holy Ghost*
elders discipline anybody's children
a homeless man knows where he is welcome
my Mother gives him some food and clothing
he rest a while on the porch, then goes on his way
"Don't be afraid to help out the tramp," says my Mother
"no one human being is better than the other"

Grandma Lessie, the Cherokee Indian

I was four years old when the trip occurred
from Wilson County, to the city of Norfolk
I stood in the doorway of Grandma's bedroom
she didn't realize that I was standing there
quietly up to her bedside, I took a closer look
Grandma Lessie, I was very curious to know
whom Daddy talked about so much
Now, imagining what other things to explore
A buzzing sound came from the kitchen
vapor flowed from the opened refrigerator door
I had never seen blocks of ices in a tray, before
and stood there, curiously thinking
How different that icebox looks from ours back home!
imagining the little blocks of ices smelled so nice
Taking another peep at my Grandma, still asleep
not seeing her eyes, I went back to exploring
a visit I was too young to hold the full memory of
but would remember the imaginary smell
of the little blocks of ices
the sound of the buzzing icebox
lying in bed sound asleep, was Grandma Lessie
the first and last time I ever saw Grandma Lessie
she looked fragile, peaceful, snoring so nice
her long black wavy *good* hair was so messy

In the Process

Farming meant beginning the full day's work in the early morn
Daddy sewed and plowed crops of tobacco, cotton, potatoes and corn
Ma had a passion for tending her vegetable and flower garden
Late Summertime was picking cotton, cropping tobacco and *barning*
processing buttermilk, churning butter and processing dried apples
a family pass time was going on berry hunts and going fishing
fresh water fish, made a meal for breakfast, dinner and for supper
Late Autumn was the time for grading tobacco ready for marketing
the season ended with *hog killing time, like a big backyard cook out*
farm neighbors customarily helped with all that work here and about
disjointing hogs for preservation, preparing good *food to eat presently*
chopped barbeque, corn on the cob, coleslaw and lemonade
men got high on corn liquor, adding fun from a hard way of living
all the good food to eat, included *home churned ice cream, a special treat!*
Hog killing time was over, Daddy joined the gentlemen on a deer hunt
A special family reward was a bus ride to the amusing County Fair
Daddy prepared the hog hams to be cured in the smoke house
Ma canned vegetables and fruits, especially for the Winter months
In the Winter months, women gathered to help *quilt bed cover*
Day's before Christmas, Daddy and family members, by mule and
wagon, went to the woods to cut down a pine tree to decorate
The time to bond and share, while the farming duties were relieved
In our house the American flag *stayed put* above the mantelpiece

Daddy the Multi-crafted

Daddy was known by farm neighbors as the *Jack-of-all-trades*
he acknowledged his Indian heritage as a proud Cherokee
high school band members could rely on Daddy's skill
to repair their damaged drums with strong durable cowhide
once he built a two-room playhouse in the back yard
my sister and I played in it joyously, until we so sadly said
"Daddy turned our playhouse into his tool shed!"
Seated by the fireplace, he rekindled with the poker
peanuts in shells on the hearth, he always *roasted um* just right
he liked to tell that same old tale, *The White Horse in the Night*
pipe tobacco smoke circulated, while he sat chipping on wood
shaping together a puppet doll, another one of his hobbies
reweaving the rocking chair, was another skill he understood
Getting in from a weekend off from the heavy farming toil
he approached the front yard, making his usual cheerful sound
a tune from his harmonica, or his favorite whistling rhyme
Daddy occasionally paid a visit to the Holiness Church
a congregation of intense shouting and dancing hallelujah!
his strong drumbeats added a dynamic sound to the band
the synchronizing with the piano, tambourines, the organ
Daddy usually a jovial man, at times could get pretty fiery
very naturally gifted, he made good use of his creativity
that was far beyond the ordinary, or the necessity for living
entertaining by the fireplace, picking on the guitar strings
from the beat of his heart came the rhythm of passion
inclined to perform on his own stage as his own person

The Magical Path

My sister Ger and I were inseparable playmates
racing each other down to what seemed like a magical path
allowing our emotions to run free, I always got there first
our typical childhood spats could wait till later
along the path, we arranged colorful wild flowers into little bouquets
we did handclapping rhymes, sang, danced and acted silly
funny face reflections added drama to the small pond of calm water
we sat down underneath the apple tree and ate a mellow apple
our favorite make-believe character was a pretty lady name *Miss Elliot*
"I'm *Miss Elliot*!" Ger said it first, but that was okay
I thought Ger fit the profile of *Miss Elliot,* she was prettier than me
we took our make-believe characters quite seriously
racing one another back to the house, as usual, I got there first
and I did a somersault, with my energetic self
Ma, with a wide brim straw hat on, was tending her vegetable garden
"Yall might run up on a snake, keep running down that weedy path"
I still love mellow apples
and true sisterly love does not diminish through the years

Hostess of the Class Picnic

The anticipated trip day finally arrived
a typical Carolina blue graced the sky
the yard was trimmed up and swept spotless
grape punch with crushed ice was ready
I was insecure about this happening
Fourth grade classmates were checking out
my country surroundings, to my surprise
I found my best friend Roberson, very amusing
I could not believe, how she was so joyously
finding the farm animals interesting
At lunchtime we ate side by side
away from the focus of so much attention
the vegetables and flower garden amazed her
mischievous gossip went on between us
Mrs. Daniels, our teacher had staged this picnic
not by my permission, but by my parents
on top of that, being persuaded by classmates
how could I have said no?
classmates responded with warm respect
a little less insecure was I, trapped as the hostess

Springtime Celebration

The flagpole wrapped in blending colors
crepe paper strips with ribbons and bows
in the middle of the high school yard
a gathering of neighbors each one knows
well groomed elementary school children
beaming huge smiles, so happy to be there
dressed in beautiful crepe paper costumes
passionately created with quality and care
a well practiced talented performance
a selection of dances around the flagpole
draws parents and neighbors together
conversations and the tasty refreshments
a springtime celebration time well spent
a well put together *Annual May Day Event*

Grandma Essie's Choir

"No more spending Saturday nights at Grandma's house
we whispered mean things about her … but not all the time
in front of her face, we were always the perfect children
guess we couldn't be the little saints like we should
no more Grandma's breakfast, shame on me for being *so wrong*
Grandma turned her back, my pancakes went out to little dog
Grandma sure kept our robes washed, starched and ironed
that evening we grand children were about to go in church
I being so busy as usual, stumbled right over the trash can
lucky for me Grandma had no time to scold
the neighbors next door got me all cleaned up
I sang like never before, keeping from spoiling things
We liked poking fun of Miss Marion, playing the piano by ear
she missed a few keys… we snickered and sang off key
we meant no harm … just fun :.. help us Lord if you please
Now … no more Grandma, her life is done, no more fun
no more practicing the songs… no more Grandchildren choir
"Grandma's funeral sure is big! Folk just keep a coming in here!"
I became touched, missing Grandma so much!

Respect the Elders

Back in the day, youngsters were told
to respect the elders, for living long
for growing old
the elders wisdom of yesterday
applies for today and for always
This is for the elders
take your rightful place
you walked the mile, you deserve to smile
your saving grace paved the way
to a better day
This is for the youth, respect the elders
for all they've been through
appreciate the elders for living long
the life of a song

The Shy Teenager Becomes the Star

A shy teenager in high school was I
my best friend Mabel, was usually by my side
in the sewing class, we made on our dresses
together, putting fourth our best effort
Attending the *Student Annual Fashion Show*
we felt good about the final creativity
and we modeled the pose appropriately
With that tall sports playing boy on my mind
on the evening of the *High School Social*
he held the doors as a courtesy, as was assigned
as I entered, he actually flirted with me
I got his approval, I was looking pretty!
later on we danced together, rather closely
he walked me home and smiled bye bye
at least for a while he was my guy
The Senior Class Play called *Gown of Glory*
was advertised at the *Downtown Theater*
my name was highlighted as *The Star*
and with the interest of *the most popular boy*
"life for me could not behold no better joy!"

First Love

My first love was so popular
just to be seen with this guy
girls seem to have no regrets
the handsome basketball star
I never, ever wanted to forget
the time he walked me home
underneath clear starlight sky
we gazed into teasing eyes
arm in arm we kissed a while
affection we shared together
the walk was only for a mile
my first love was really fine
the problem he wasn't mines
for he could make a choice
any girl – any kind – no fret
still my kind of guy, you bet
the love I would never forget

The Most Exciting City
1956

In New York! New York! there's massive transit
subways, cars, taxies, buses, walkers, bikers
the sound of horns steadily honking aggressively
amazing how jammed up traffic starts to flow
the sidewalk is crowded with a great many people
a lot of them, with no particular place to go
42nd Street – different races – the melting pot
shoppers are holding onto the purchased goods
just taking some safety precautions, *if you would*
it's always convenient to get something to eat
vendors by numbers are set up along the street
Another fabulous performance is taking place
down at the Time Square Broadway Theater
the most famous music hall, Radio City
Sightseeing goes on along New York Harbor
the Empire State Building, the Statue of Liberty
tourist are photographing the beautiful view
famous skyscrapers, just to mention a few
believe it or not, this country girl has fallen in love
with the New York Style, glamorous and trendy
her goal is to become a fashion designer
in New York! New York! the most exciting city!

Jam Session

The Jam session is alive
couples are dressed
in a trendy style
acquaintances are special
regulars are feeling fine
making lively conversation
casually drinking
whatever the preference
displaying sophistication
a laidback atmosphere
grooving to the beat
jazz rhythm is diverse
smooth and unique
"there is a party going on!"
at the popular night spot
the jam session is hot!

Down Home Party in the City

The down home party in the city
the atmosphere of *bonding with my people*
homies are drinking pretty hardy
the notorious big talkers and laughter
always standing out at the party
who else but the *North Carolinians*
soul music is turned up to capacity
homies are crowded all over the place
not a whole lot of space to dance
dancing is going on anyhow!
time… not a concern…just let it fly
fogs of cigarette smoke, not a concern
just let the liquor keep rolling
don't let the crispy fried chicken burn!
potato salad and coleslaw, on the platter
homies from different walks of life
come together, drinking, dancing, eating
the main *down home dish is chitterlings*

On the Ballroom Floor

Partners swinging on the ballroom floor
skirts a whirling round and round
legs are on display, gentleman in control
a couple goes stealing all the attention
the crowd applauds the attraction
a country couple take to the floor
friends of theirs fall out with laughter
"ballroom daincing aint what they know!"
hilariously off the floor they go
couples a swinging all over the place
skirts a whirling legs are on display
the country couple?
will stick to what they know, *two stepping*
but not on a ballroom floor

Holding Attention

She is holding attention
dressed in all white
a sleeveless blouse and shorts
swaying barefooted
to the exotic sound
lamplight glows softly
children are on the sidewalk
passing back and forth
peering into the window
the curtains flows
calm summer breeze
she plays the sound again
holding onto her audience
gently in the moment
she kisses good bye the night
in the morning daylight
this teenager will be leaving
for summer vacation!

Branches

Reminiscing on the way to pay Auntie a visit
turned into sadness near the street where Roberson once lived
my best friend's death was too painful to talk about until now
the pretty alert girl next door was planning on going to college...
Daddy was among his coworker; I was ashamed of my Daddy
hoping he wouldn't spot me among the crowd of school children
he was much too gifted to be a *garbage man*
Debbie the youngest, did not remember our deceased Dad...
Darden High band was marching, pretty majorettes were stepping...
In the auditorium, Mr. Satchell was playing the piano passionately
and I was a part of the chorus, singing gloriously...
At *Senior Class Night*, of fun and mischievous discoveries
the shy *bobby-socker* as I, was elected the *1955 Most Friendliest Girl*
never perceived myself as exceptionally friendly ... *Who me?*
my shapely legs, *as were described* had been *humorously willed*
a junior class girl was named, as *the proud recipient...*
Only yesterday, it seemed, I trod that path... how times changed!
living in NY, held a different branch of experiences
a simple walk in Wilson, with my sister Debbie
became a special time to probe into the past
recapturing *good old days* of the country value of simplicity
to free my soul from *suppressed grief and shame*

Romantically Inclined

1950's, me at age 21, in my home at Brooklyn New York.

Desire

It's sheer magic within the moment
but for the future, concerning this affair
the seriousness behind the laughter
does he even care?
I need commitment, more than a lover
he has a playful hint of recklessness
is he playing with my heart
with this incredible profile of *his highness*
with someone else, when we are apart ?
not sure I'm ready for an answer
that perhaps could spoil the ecstasy
we have something in common
opposites attract, he is real, so am I
do we have what it takes to make it last?
or does he even care?
As though reading my mind, he whispers
"In the moment, let's just take it slow
enjoy the source, to handle our differences
will have to take its course…
I like being side by side with you!"
our favorite love song agreed, and I did too
When we are together, exchanging laughter
music and love songs surrounds
what does he truly feel
the moment after we both feel so alive?
my desire, this affair will forever survive

Warm December Days

Right from the start of our acquaintance
our eyes were in touch with the truth of our souls
love, based not on the future but for the moment
we laughed aloud until time got in the way
to embrace what our hearts once tried to deny
our love like sunshine warming the December days
Along the way we lost sight of the harmony
singing my version of the romantic song
but by the beat of his drum and rhythm off key
until the early morn we dreamed about each other
we harmonized once again under the moon
and then his lyrics fell completely out of tune
O yes, we would rather laugh at life than frown
for life owed us happiness yesterday and now
we took time out to be together as time passed by
and it came the time to go our separate ways
the memory of our romance will last eternally
the love that warmed the December days

Single Mom

Society is experiencing a social change
by the humanitarian plight for equal rights
women are making a stand for liberation
this breadwinner's salary does not measure up
inflation is rising, discrimination still exist
having to defend my dark skin, when will it end?
going from one job to the other, a job laid off
a job cut back, the next one out of business
which means I have no long-term job security
I will not allow this government supplementary
income to define my mentality
I'm using sewing skills for an in-home business
and leading the children to the church
to get involved in Christian activities
to be in the presence of the faithful members
to cherish friendships offering a helping hand
I'm rather youthful, fairly attractive
needing *Mr. Right* along comes *Mr. Wrong*
negative attention I can live without
a good man is like a needle in a hay-stack
I'm human, I get lonely for companionship
yet refuse to be any man's sex object
I can face the true reality of my circumstances
I will uphold my standards of self-respect

Spoken in Time

This relationship is going to be for real
so says you only…well this is the right time
to let you know just how I feel
just so we don't waste time with each other
in an involvement only getting tougher
already you are pulling my strings
like I'm your toy...you got it all wrong
it takes two, to share the joy
your self centered approach leaves me in doubt
the proper time for romance
is what I'm all about…I am *self-assured*
you are much too controlling
together you and me?… not meant to be

My Dream Man

This observant man, compliments me
a man with a pleasing sense of humor
a romantic lover, a spiritual man
concerned about the needs of others
This amazing man, faithful and true
our relationship embodies respect
this special man appreciates me
as a special lady, cool and unique
the man I can count on as a friend
criticizes and disagrees constructively
he is the character of the man I need
discovering the very same in me
Nothing is too good for the man I love
heaven sent him to me from above
it's pleasing to look into his face
being with this man, I don't need space
we know how love is suppose to feel
this wonderful man I am thinking of
is a *dream* of my man being real

Temptation

He was the visiting minister at my church
and I was in need of a special friend
this charming man went seriously pursuing me
friendly conversation proceeded
to take the acquaintance to another level
intimately he offered, to be untrue...to his wife
he was a married man
Phone conversations followed in this direction
he wanted us to be the best of friends
he wanted to show his affection
a hand to me, he would be glad to lend
no one else would have to know
about the secluded vacations we could go
I responded quite true and direct,
" I cannot be the other woman to a married man"
"I am a minister, he replies, I have to
put up with my wife, it goes against ministry
to get a divorce, I have to live with the strife."
"Spiritual places you must pursue... *for the Lord*
you have a wife and the strife
I have my freedom and refuse to settle for less
goodbye my love, I will not be your mistress!"

Love Slipped Away

The day the gentleman and I got acquainted
I did not connect with those charming eyes
I was too uninterested to be lured by that smile
Wanting to get to know me much better
he refused to give up, until we would get together
after several dates, seriously checking him out
he turned out to be a pretty cool gentleman
we continued to date like a real couple
he needed for us to be more than just friends
yet nothing more had changed on my behalf
a relationship with this gentleman I could not see
I needed time, but too much time passed by
this gentleman gave up on a relationship with me
Days followed, I missed his loyal company
those charming eyes gave only me the attention
without him any longer, was out of the question
It must not be too late, to get back with my guy
my guy had found someone new, to connect
with his eyes, now I needed to connect with too
with nothing more to say, "I let love slip away!"

Intimate Attraction

The gentleman just took me by surprise
he continued to flirt so smoothly with me
yet intimacy between such age differences
I surely could not see
he and I together could only be a fantasy
affectionate expressions became quite bold
seemingly not meant for someone too old
"Maybe I should check this young man out
for differences can lift two people higher
involved with a younger man? Not my desire
a relationship destined to clash
high on a pedestal, only to take a backlash"
Observing this young man's masculinity
became clear to see what he saw in me
not a number, but a lively personality
all along there had been a true chemistry
between different levels of maturity
Harmless flirtation became, pretty neat!
work day moments became, pretty sweet!

Bring Back Romance

Yesterday, amid the good
the pretty, the bad, the ugly
there was love to dream of
to make magical and real
a wonderful emotion
no one today, seem to feel
Romance was in your life
then suddenly disappeared
so hold your head up high
for you are as important
as the next human being
bring out the best of you
accept not just anything
in more ways than one
romance can come again

Blossoms

I Will Honor the Memory of Junior
9-2-1967.....7-27-1993

Caring around the grief over the death of my son
seems forever trapped in endless distress
like noisy chaos within my conscious
for God's help I'm crying out, I can't do this alone
my son is dead, I cannot deny, he will not come back
I will honor the memory of my son who was dear
still I feel stuck in this roller coaster frame of mind
reality seems like an out of body experience
either I will rise above this ordeal, moment by moment
or the moments will press too heavy on my heart
Lord, I will surrender this grief for Your direction
I have the assurance, You are hearing my cry
being robbed of my son is something that I resent
discouragement is hindering my will to accept this
through this path of darkness, I will utilize faith
to place my grief upon until the day of solace

A Flower

The blossoming of the flower
there comes the time
the vitality of the flower
is cut short and fade away
In time there will be tranquility
to calm the sweltering pain
of missing the liveliness
of the beloved spirit
Yet the faded flower
from time to time will blossom
anew, with liveliness of spirit
within the mind
The bouquet takes its place
the room comes alive
I think of the lively spirit
and I smile

Within the Course of Time

Images of the past still lasting into the presence
setting sunlight peeps between branches of tall trees
an unpainted church house stands amid clay colored grass
a poet crafts the language of this countryside scenery
preserved through decades in the same place of serenity
First steps are taken into a great world to explore
a dramatic developer, surrounded by many expressions
in a world that likes to laugh at curious discoveries
walking on its own, and creating sentimental memories
the innocence of youth steps onto a stage of immaturity
And time itself becomes a readily true companion
the reminder of the reality emerging through potentials
the advisor of decisions, choices, and consequences
time's provisions of consciousness just gets in the way
of the invincible minded, before immaturity is heightened
Arriving on time, but much too soon, the *Senior*
with a host of life lessons, through a time of experiences
must turn yet to the inner child, to face a new world
a new generation, applying the golden rule, the same
how time goes by, how soon, the seasons change

Portrait

The Creator of the land abide above in heaven
as well as in the richness of the earth below
the Creator walk not in a designated space
nor chooses to remain only in a specific place
Given the mind to follow either way to go
humans not always follow the way of the lamb
wouldn't it be wonderful if humans would know
how to fit more love into the Creator's program
The Creator sculptured a wondrous world
provisions of mountains, oceans, and rivers
the seasons with all of the magnificent
a work of perfection for all of the inhabitants
The earth behold the extraordinary of all sorts
especially for the painter to exercise the brush
by a mystical approval of clouds floating by
a picturesque landscape beneath the sky
Animals of the wilderness, supplied with needs
the wondrous things of the sea; all of the species
the heaven up above with angels truly perfect
all things blend in the Creator's amazing portrait

The Time is Right

To pursue my dream? not right now, I am much too young
this dream can wait, until tomorrow for now, I'll just have fun

With youthfulness, and my dream, the race, I'm willing run
when my dreams become a reality, my life will have just begun

Because of the color of my skin, I cannot pursue my dream
I don't feel much acceptance, and that's the sad state I'm in

The obstacles will always be around, to always get in the way
by making my dream come true, I will make it a better day

My dream, is only a fantasy, I am not good looking you see
society worships beauty, and where does that leave me?

Appearance is not an excuse to whine, I will pursue my dream
inward beauty, flows outward, from this soul of mines

My dream cannot come true, success is not based on being poor
I cannot pursue without the funds, how can I open any door?

There's no point sitting around wasting time, wondering how?
I will increase my employment; I will not know until I try

Society's preference is for the young, I'm left out in the cold
my thoughts are not on a dream, it is too late, I am much to old

I'm putting to use my wisdom, ability, drive, and creativity
the time is right, to make the challenge, the answer is up to me

To Carry a Song

Desires are many, the surrounding are plentiful
sing a thankful melody for big or small prosperity
a melody for whatever the day may bring
if ever there comes a time, when hope seems gone
a joyful song, uplifts the will to carry on
Meditate as a way of life, to face the world
to make peace with the storm of different forms
reconcile with acceptance of diversity in humanity
with faith in God to guide the days
meditations emerges as a glorious song of praise
Don't forget to be thankful for the sunshine
the nighttime, the moon and stars, in the sky above
stay humble beneath God's wrath, His love
to bring out the best of you, and hope and pray
to bring out the best of someone else
for we live in a world, not alone, all by ourselves
Desires are many, the surroundings are plentiful
a thankful melody, is for big are small prosperity
a melody for whatever the day may bring
if ever there comes a time, when hope seems gone
a joyful song, uplifts the will to carry on

Omen of Stability

With no choice but to listen
to the raging storm in orbit, heavy thunder
pouring rain, electrifying lightening
the wind sounds a harsh rumbling language
turning into a singing fury of displeasure
consciously, "God is in charge!"
the storm took a calming effect, a welcome relief
yet in a split second
violent wind destined on into the night
as I listened to the roaring ceaseless energy
Everything was silent…was this a dream?
In fear to the window, in the morning time
sunlight peeped through dark rolling clouds
the massive storm had decreased
branches and debris drifted over the floodwater
an astonishing thing caught my eye
onto a thin limb of a tree
a small birdhouse was swinging gently
in the now, calm wind, like an omen of stability

Dialogue

No one can define the feelings of another
but to lend a listening ear for understanding
When family members cannot express
the innermost feelings to each other
or listen to the truth from one another's soul
how sad when judgments or assumptions
becomes defining factors of the characters
and that's so wrong to pass on as generational
Favoritism in a family stands in the way
of the overall unity in the family
when a natural compatible relationship exist
free from spreading rift among the others
then the others are magnetized
to that *role model* display of leadership
Respectfully sharing inner emotions
compassionate towards each other's pain
being conversational, exchanging opinions
no two people have to feel the same
getting to know more about the character
of the other, it's called, "dialogue"
Blame just creates some major blame
communication in the meaningful direction
is the key to the end of a pressing situation
the conflict, no longer out of control
peace in the family is guided by "dialogue"

And Life Moves On

Picture frames speaks volumes
embodies the personality
relating with the times
It's good to reminisce
sentimental memories
to keep a thoughtful account
of meaningful experiences
but keep it real, life moves on
sing the classic song
but never all day long
Yesterday's happenings
bares fruits of valuable lessons
to live by, in the presence

To Follow the Heart

No longer under the shadows
of dominating expectations
the courage has finally been gained
to challenge personal convictions
experiences have taken its toll
dismissals have played its games
determination has been conquered
things are no longer the same
no longer vulnerable to judgments
fulfilled by a new creation
now focused on a free direction
and setting priorities in order
not by the mind of some other
no baggage from yesterday
but to follow the heart triumphantly!
Though life bestow not always
the friends, but must face the foes
yet both the voices bares reasons
to consider free will choices
to follow the heart triumphantly

Education for All Time's Sakes

Equal Education for our children
determines not by skin color or race
but by our minds being in the right place
Calling All:
Parents, Students, Teachers, Preachers
Boards of Education, The Church
The Village, Policy Makers, Legislators
offer a concerned support for adequate
education, all children included, for
each child has a natural need to learn
in a school without low expectations
but to learn by the proper alternative
We in this together, the old, the young
the in-between, all with caring hearts
for our children to succeed
for the sake of the colors of the generations
recognize the sunflowers abiding amidst the weeds

Light of Yesterday

Hopefully a child will grow upright
by the guiding light along the way
the offering of strong supportive hands
through the child becoming of age
when it seems like the sudden wind
blows away the youthful innocence
The youth will turn to negative choices
will go in some wrong directions
will listen to some misleading voices
will explore some bad experiences
as the guiding light keeps on shining
over youth out of control aggressions
The youth will grow into maturity
will brace up and take responsibility
out of a greater need to live right
to take a more positive view of things
and look back on the invincible way
to see light of today shone yesterday

Anti – Aging?

Ageing begins with conception
the process of life 'til death
cosmetic surgery?
can not stop the years from passing
for the sake of young people
the role of the parent is to be exemplary
of the approach to the stages of life
as to nourish the mental growth
to satisfy the thirst for rational thinking
to nourish the physical growth
with overall good health practices
to nourish the spiritual growth
with the grace of self- acceptance

Something in Common

The wealthy community of high level- success
professionals, business people, the career driven
prestigious mentalities, seem can do no wrong
yet there exist both the weak and the strong
The middle class community, thriving fruitfully
environmental appearance of financial stability
those who belong to the weak and the strong
The working poor, just struggling to get by
the insufficient income does not meet the needs
of higher hopes to challenge, the dreams to succeed
In this abundant world, the poor are degraded
the poor carries a heavy burden to bear, the
scapegoat profile, nobody of society, deserve to wear
back in the day, as my grandmother would put it:
"until you walk on my journey, don't bother me!"
Imagine a world without the people who cares
give thanks for people doing abundance of deeds
in a world of many children suffering in need
those who belong to the weak and the strong

Fruits of Creativity

There's more than meets the eye
a fine quality deep within to discover
to give a new endeavor a try
the nourishment, a kind of work
is therapeutic, exciting, fulfilling
to nourish to a level of esteem
A strong wind sings its songs out loud
seasons embraces its colors on time
when inner creativity develops into sight
oneself evolves to a greater height

Let Justice Intervene

So you developed a song and dance routine
by imitating the unique artistry of someone else
by your popularity rather than true talent
crazed fans by the millions
creating a mega fantasy of stardom, out of your name
you rose above to fortune and fame
surpassing the other artist, now to you never exist
who you deviated from giving due courtesy and respect
whose unique style landed you *on top of the list*
The song of some other, is a song to sing,
dance moves are for those who choose, *but here's the thing*
true talent develops by imagination
yet, another artist.originality may truly be inspirational
Justice is a part of freedom of speech, song and dance
that didn't seem to occur to you
while relentlessly imitating your American Dream
you failed to allow justice to intervene

Beautiful Dark Skin Female

Beautiful dark skin sister, you are a star!
do not accept the shunning of your skin
never mind what society may think
turn this thing around, beauty is personal
based not on a carbon copy, but one of a kind
Your natural beauty lies within your genes
so appreciate the melanin in your skin
work with it, with facials, better eating habits
fresh fruits, raw or cooked vegetables
Think not of yourself as inferior
by the wrong messages constantly spreading
you are not the most unhealthy of them all
beauty applies to a new prospective on you
take care of yourself, your overall being
this applies also to my *Senior Sister*
you are a shining star! You are a Queen!

Handling Business

Gossiping about the affairs of someone else
character attacking with false accusations
creating drama, being judgmental, creating strife
boldly envious towards someone's appearance
a sad soul who gossips, need to get a life
As the instigators take the center of attention
the vicious cycle keep right on spreading
"swallowing my self esteem will not digest
I added not a word to the malice
I outsmarted the nonsense with confidence!"
The lovers as well as the haters are existing
caring is heard on the voices of lovers
and on the faces contentment shows
the haters are blinded by self-hatred the most
Respect the child, the man, the woman
respect the friend, the coworkers, the elders
the key first and foremost is to respect oneself

To Hold the Interest

Some people talk very little
other's just chatter away
it's not about how much you talk
it's all about what you say
one man gave a speech in a half hour
the other man's speech seemed half-a-day
some people will avoid talking
for others that's never okay
delivering speech patterns varies
some people speak a great vocabulary
for others, big words never pay
some people talk junk about people
whoever comes their way
it's not about how much you talk
it's all about what you say

Differences

Perceptions are not always the same…
two people are listening to music
hearing the melody quite differently
observing the same painting
with differences of perceptions
attending a great sports event
cheering by personal preference
pondering over wonderful poetry
literary views don't have to rhyme
compatible twosome?
only when based on the fact
that two people have the ability
to engage in conversation
to argue through differences
and still have the other one's back
opinions don't have to be the same
the relationship remains in tack

Colorless Emotions

The shade of the skin, the features
of the face, the texture of the hair
the color of the eyes, the soul of the person
too many people seem not to see – or care
such views are obstructive to unity
To form a negative opinion of someone
because of the difference in color or race
those prejudice attitudes of today
are simply out of place
no one have the right to look down
on the unfortunate of the universe
any one's life can take a turn for the worst
For each of us to remain equal and free
as the human race desire to be
stand not in the way of humanity
black, white, brown, yellow colors the skin
is this where the perception of someone's
emotions begin and end?

Where's the Person?

The white person
the black person

the skinny person
the fat person

the rich person
the poor person

the old person
the young person

communication…
shut down!

everything was seen
but the person!

Steadfast Inspiration

"Hello, I haven't seen you for a long time
as time went by, I could never forget you
I am positive you haven't a clue
Finally, I have the chance to let you know
something you did became a part of me also
As you took time out to pray in a very solemn way
I was reminded to exercise my faith
with a daily prayer for the rest of my days

Needing More

So much time gone by, without reaching my goal
I haven't become all I desire to be, expect to achieve
fate does not matter, I have my heart and soul to follow
to bring out the very best of me, whatever time relates
the need to gain accomplishment, time itself creates
In rhythm like an eagle, to conquer mountains galore
taking on the challenge, spreading my wings to soar
on the way to the end results, approval commitment makes
to unlock the door to fulfillment, intent is what it takes
chasing desires through winding roads, changing times
to reach my destination, at times it seems much too far
I'm focused on the prize; gone too far to turn around
I must satisfy my need, to prove myself to me
then for love ones and friends, even for the public to see
In a rhythm like an eagle, over mountains, I am going
with anticipation, I'm spreading my wings and soaring

Mishaps

Mishaps will happen
that's life as they say
an annoying obstacle
just get in the way
the same old mishap
over and over again
hinders good progress
prevents effectiveness
mishaps much too often
each time gives a clue
examine the dysfunction
there's rethinking to do
mishaps will happen
as blessings in disguise
at the end of the mishaps
is where the blessings lie
Carelessly performing
un-orderly way of living
in need of a solution
try organized thinking

Evolving by Faith

Looking forward for a dream to come true
takes heart and soul and the frame of mind
to appreciate the vision, each moment of time
a challenge at times comes under restraint
other obligations overshadows the imagination
Ordeals intervene at times irreversible
the unexpected dampens the will to keep trying
what feels like no ending to the pain
to calm down discouragement seems useless
the challenge is now faced with a greater test
Who knows the outcome of the future
things can go so right, then suddenly go wrong
like a beautiful song suddenly sung off key
yet the reason to sing remains the same
a God given gift appreciated, is never in vain
To go on challenging a dream to come true
takes heart and soul and the frame of mind
natural creativity quite naturally gets hard
yet to keep looking forward to the day of reward

Divine Intervention Through the Clutter of the Conscious

Imagine a World

Free from racism… favoritism…classism
is that a unrealistic thought to hard to even imagine?
we as human beings are vulnerable to danger
One's race does not make anyone superior or invincible
can a human view just replace a bias view?
Favoritism is not even necessary to practice among the children
but to view the children as individuals
and to be truly available to reach each child's needs
to show positive concern about each child's behavior patterns
Classism means looking down on the less fortunately
not a smart thing to do
Imagine a world without racism…favoritism…classism
is to imagine a world through the eyes of
humanity... individuality... character
Is that realistic?

Adding to the Glory

The choice of belief
is by the free will of the believer
I believe in Jesus Christ
as the Lord and Savior
the teacher of righteousness
into the spirit of those
who accept His guide and glory
not according to class, race
or financial category
Amazing grace prepares growth
of spirituality
to enlighten the mind
to reject society's dictations
of how one should feel
about oneself, in relations
to worldly things
To become conscientiously aware
of how to share
not only material things
but spiritual support, physical
emotional support, the
provisions as blessings above
all material possessions

The Promise

God placed Adam and Eve in the garden of Eden
they ate the forbidden fruit, disobeyed God's command
sin among human beings, became prevalent in the land
characterized by vulnerability to hurt harm and danger
even the very young may be vulnerable to tragedy
The son of God was crucified on the Cross of Calvary
and His resurrection gave human beings the chance
to be born again, as the way to a relationship with Him
The redemption experience first and foremost is by faith
desire to turn from sin, to submit to Jesus forgiveness
often times, a destructive path, leads to applying the faith
the way to a repentance, to beseech His everlasting grace
God never promised me a bed of roses, but the redeemer
my sins were forgiven by the amazing grace of Jesus
no longer led by the natural will, but by the spiritual will
to keep my part of the promise, to follow His light
through days and nights, to be obedient in His sight

The Friend I Needed the Most

Jesus Christ, the blessed, merciful prince of peace
taught me how to live with a brand new sight
by amazing grace, I learned to see the light
I would not go another day being discontented
depending on somebody else to bring me happiness
Looking towards Heaven, I prayed to Jesus Christ
He understood, I needed a change in my life
to willingly submit to Him, without hesitation
guided by the Holy Spirit over my imperfections
feeling His presence, I surrendered my sins
By His forgiveness, my soul became redeemed
He led me to believers who gave inspiration
on sustaining prayers, as the cornerstone for life
experiences of joy, as well as the complications
to depend on the blessed savior Jesus Christ
Jesus Christ became the friend I needed the most
the humble child of God of superior wisdom
to see imperfections as room for spiritual growth
I am so glad, of the day He came into my life
by His amazing grace, I learned to see the light

Something in Life to Believe in

Through my conviction
to pursue a passion
self-pity at times comes in the way
of true value
the world does not always recognize
so busy placing the lesser original
upon a pedestal
At times I have to tell myself
It's okay to cry
the world is not the comforter
of my self-pity
the world can be deliberately
so unfair and cold
By Your sovereign providence
O Lord replenish my soul
I must fulfill this need
to succeed, by strengthening
my faith... in me
crossing over the barriers
setting my vision free
upholding the will to win
leaning on the everlasting arms
"the something in life to believe in"

Facing the Demons

You make sure to be around
sneaking up on your own time
you cannot exist on your own
you cannot leave folk alone
you show up in many faces
yet you are one in the same
playing the same sly game
I have much better things to do
than to keep my mind on you
I don't play games, I think
by my rule, by my own time
you will keep your space
for sure, I will keep mines
I'm glad I know who I am
you don't fit into my program
your helpers are just like you
playing games, on the run
I can also face your little demons

Lord I Am in Need to Feel Your Love

O Lord, I am in need for Your love
Your superior power so high above
many things seem to be falling apart
I am loosing control of peace at heart
I realize Lord, everyday Your love is free
today I am not feeling the harmony
complications just keep blinding my way
I am constantly praying You hear me say
I am in need to feel Your love today
To figure out a solution is much too consuming
when troubles keep piling up way to high
lead me back to the glory of Your beam
shower down the solution from above the sky
please don't leave me in this state alone
Show me the clearer way make me strong
I was dancing along and lost my step
to dance once again Lord, I need Your help

On Behalf of the Elderly and the Poor

America, the land of many immigrants
people taking a proud in their individual race
but those who assume, any other group as inferior
those superior attitudes, have no rightful place
cannot heal by written laws on paper
but must heal, by a moral approach to society
To be defined by great success is quite natural
the wealthy is morally blessed also
if not to steal from the elderly and the poor
America will become an even greater country
when the greatness becomes consistent
with the practice of equality, in overall society
equal education, equal hiring practices
fair housing, equal business opportunity
Numerous poor people are more than willing
to pull themselves up, by the boot straps
they don't want to be profiled as *all the same*
it's not right for them to be judged, or viewed
as though they are the *scapegoats of society*
they need job security, equal work, equal pay
the very same things most Americans need
a fair chance to achieve financial success
the chance to achieve the American Dream
Together we can make America a greater country
based on a moral approach to one another

Victory

The athlete is warming up with readiness
just minutes before taking on the challenge
meditating on self discipline with confidence
emotionally well prepared to master the opponent
physically fit to go straight toward the finish line
the focus is set to go...off goes the signal
off goes the amazing speed seeming so easy
gaining momentum, greatly driven to victory – yes!
Dedicated sportsmanship, a perfect performance
the strong will to succeed displays a similarity
to spiritual survival, by faith to persevere
to challenge emotional weakness and heavy rejection
even the greatest gift of all sustains by practice
to over power the opposition, courageously
the spiritual will, reaches the expected victory – yes!

My Pledge to Thee

Through the fertility of my spirituality
my growth become stagnant, but set in order
by the chastising from the Lord and Savior
to keep free from irrational thinking
An intricate part of daily activity is praying
resting upon the pillows of my faith
I fast and prayed in secrecy with the Lord
for nourishment of humbleness of spirit
to continue the developing by the edification
O Lord I know you are my refuge
I know I need to grow more disciplined
to prayerfully live upright in Your providence
I will praise Your name, merciful Savior
the Holy Spirit, always there for me

Love is Enough

Love may not mold a child into all of your desires
love is enough by the will
give all the love that you can give
If you care anything about your parents
your sister, your brother, love is enough by the will
give all the love you can give
If you have the heart and desire
let your light shine brighter, lend someone a hand
realize, you too is sure to need a helping hand
before the day is through
Pray that a friend will stay around a little while
until your trouble will subside
Bring more love into this land
give a helping hand, love is enough by the will
give all the love that you can give
If you don't know how to love, look to Heaven above

War or Peace?

Who will solve the problem
created by a number of dictators
who can avoid the conflict
by visualizing the horrors
of innocent lives being lost
who will pay the cost?
After ruins and so much waste
did the problem reach a better place
did destruction of yesterday
heal the ills of today
did the weapons right the wrong
when the conflict raged along?
What should cease, war or peace?
Why not face the fears
to avoid violence and tears
reasoning can be rewarding
what should cease, war or peace?

Bonding Power

Children are bonding at play on a regular basis
playing sports, loosing, winning, dancing
and singing, spending less time at the TV screen
video games, not the most interesting things
bonding families are gathered at the dining table
out in the yard, leisurely walking in the park
holding conversations, getting back to the basics
On the other hand, the main source of socializing
the instant way at any distance, time or place
is looking through the windows of technology
taking the place of communicating and bonding
through the eyes as the windows to the soul
In this global technological world of information
personal affairs of others are easily discovered
folks miss out on getting to know one another

A Direct Approach to Life

The future is always beyond
ambitions on the mind to pursue
the presence is always the time
to make those dreams come true
Learn from the past experiences
the great lesson that gives advice
put the lesson into practice
take a direct approach to life
To worry about the unknown
hinders dealing with the known
do the absolute best right now
while the ability moves on and on
Be prepared in the very moment
from this very point of view
allow a direct approach to life
begin right now to work for you

The Storms of Life

The storms of life
unrest injurious
young becomes old
and the strain is furious

The storm ceases
bruises are healed
roots are sprouting
and the budding is revealed

Old becomes young
new life takes room
a day in sunshine
and the flower is in bloom

Patience the Ultimate Emotion

Patience is easy to see and to define
above emotional feelings of all kinds
patience will bare with one's own self
patience will bare with somebody else
emotional feeling can become disguised
patience is right before the very eyes
when will patience not bare with tension
will agitation become too overwhelming?
patience will determine what is useless
patience is never speechless for words
a calm spirit refuses to be misinterpreted
not a sign of weakness, but reign supreme
in control, the ultimate emotion to hold

Work Yet to be Done

The earth shook, rumbled violently, fracturing Haiti
beneath the rubble, suddenly are the dead, the dying
fatherless, motherless, kinships nowhere to be find
a body is pulled out alive from the wreckage
after hanging on through days of terror
another body, pulled out dead… a baby…dead bodies
people are wandering around in disarray
as people are tending to the wounded
through catastrophe, people are in the spirit of caring
Help from abroad finally arrives for the Haitians
will these ruins mark a new beginning for construction
to flourish, craved by Haitians for centuries, yet
plagued by poverty and corruption, now more destruction
By the resilience of the Haitians, their world is rebuilt
economical fruitful, the people are risen up with elation
Is this in God's plan for such a revelation for the Haitians?

Bridges

Alone with only the whispers of the wind
somehow I got lost, crossing over the bridge
and now, I am depending only on the company of God
and the sweet tunes of the birds, appearing in the sky
like angels passing by … Over there, I see a fig tree
something to eat... a drink of water is in the creek
the increasing sounds I hear is getting closer…and closer
there's no way to run, to stay alive!... Amazing grace
the lion is running on out of sight!
Out of nowhere, someone is here to rescue me!
I, a weary soul will survive, to go back at home
safe from danger in the woods all alone…
Yet there was gentleness in the midst of the uncertainty
the sweet fig tree; tunes from the birds in the sky
was pleasant company, and water was in the creek
I was saved mysteriously from the teeth of a lion
and rescued by a stranger… I awakened from the dream!
Now back to the reality, of surrounding things
made not with an independent mind, or hand
the hands of humanity, inhabitants of all sorts, and nature
the mysterious as well, attaches the bridges for survival
in the hand of the almighty Creator

From Greed to Prosperity

A sad part of today's society is soul unrest
inner resourcefulness many people suppress
so undiscovered by out of control greed
too often over something of little or no need
individuals can display a false sense of competing
bragging is conversationally straight to the core
no one has anything to brag about
yet everyone have something to be thankful for
Character observation is a regular need
not to worship or adorn as a special work of art
but to condition the soul, the mind, and the heart
to replace greed with the true value of living
all around for all to see, are provisions
provisions including nature, vital and free

Solutions Alarm

Greed is constantly overpowering those in need
women raising children alone, families without a home
many individuals fall prey to self-destruction
winding up in the whirlwind of criminal activity
through the revolving doors of incarceration
while networking of guns, drugs and dealers goes free
Show young children what love looks like:
spirituality – morality – compassion – integrity
leadership – common sense – intelligence – equality
To encourage a society from polarization
never enough messages can ever be spoken
not only to recite the rhythm of the verse
but to follow the message for what it is worth
Lift up one another, rather than to tear one other down
but to liberate the mind – to liberate the mind!
not only by speaking the words, but by showing
today, a liberated society is growing!
Not only to recite the rhythm of the verse
but to follow the message for what it is worth

Contents of Character

Martin Luther King had a dream that one day
his four children will not be judged
by the color of their skin
but by the contents of their character
he could very well have said: *To be judged by their*
achievements that comes by equality
because that's what the struggle was all about
but he knew first and foremost
above all struggles; above all achievements
takes character to go around the obstacles

A Prayer

A prayer out loud
or a silent prayer
I pray
A prayer indoors or outdoors
I pray
A prayer for myself
or for someone else
I pray
A prayer with others or without
I pray
each day to face my way
I pray

A Rendition of Faith to Raise Up Our Youth

Our hearts are lifted up to You O Lord of royalty
for the edification for the stages of our youth
with blessed assurance of Your guiding reverence
we are raising up our youth to stand for loyalty!
The child who has studies with the willingness to soar
the parents, as a part of the success of the child's education
gives the child a standing ovation!
Many children are impoverished, in an abundant land
in the sight of the Father in heaven
the reason is not always exposed to comprehend
yet a human countenance upon the child doing without
we are raising up our youth from all walks of life!
Our hearts are lifted up to You O Lord of royalty
we magnify the edification to raise up our youth
we are adorned in the armor of fidelity
building a foundation, on that our youth shall stand
we are together, as a great society, hand in hand
the motivators for all of our youth, beneath the sky
with blessed assurance, of Your guiding reverence
Our youth shall rise! Our youth shall rise!

I Can Tell You That I Care

I see the wonder in your eyes
the struggle to handle your desires
if it was up to me
I'd build your hopes real high
and place a ladder at your feet
to take the steps towards your sky
but to fulfill all your dreams
of victories, through tears
in life there are no guarantees
I cannot tell you life is fair
but to handle the complications
I can tell you that I care
when we talk, and with laughter
I love to see your smile
though at times, it's hard for you
to make connection with your eyes
we always seem to comprehend
the true love we share within
If it was up to me
I'd build your hopes real high
and place a ladder at your feet
to take the steps towards your sky

Values

Today's culture dictates that the main value to life
is to achieve wealth and material possessions
to worship outward beauty, whether vain or not
this perception overshadows the spiritual approach
to circumstances, whether good or the adversity
or the pain and suffering
Humans are not born with total independency
we must make the effort to share ideas, suggestions
opinions, and a generous shoulder to lean on
from time to time, a compassionate listening ear
Integrity brings out the very best of oneself
encourages the best of the other person
and compliment the beauty, deeper than the skin

Feeling the Music

I'm feeling the music of the symphony
synchronizing instruments in perfect harmony
it's my time to rise and listen to the soft melody
Through commitment and undying devotion
taking a passion on the depth of my emotions
visualizing the perfection will come to light
my soul is ready to rise to a greater height
I'm feeling the lovely music of the symphony
synchronizing instruments in perfect harmony
my time to rise and listen to the soft melody

Not Everybody Wants What Everybody Else Got

Life has a plan, if life can't teach you, no one can
you don't have to have what somebody else got
you have your own preference, taste and style
to satisfy your overall needs, may take a while
We are living in such a materialistic society
some people just can't understand how somebody
can have the common sense, or the intelligence
or the individuality, or the source of spirituality
to accept what they have, or have not achieved
until gaining a necessity, make the most of things
will begin to count blessings, will look around
at nothing to complain about, will have found
not everybody wants what everybody else got
but to change things for the better, whenever can
will be content knowing, "my life holds my plan!"

Signals

A persecutor, by the sword of harassment
attempts to tear down, a redeemed one's peace of mind
the redeemed one is tempted to attack the evil one
with an exchange of harassment also
and the Lord restrains the redeemed one not to do so
The disciplined behavior of the redeemed is blessed
while the persecutor ways remain in wickedness
refuses to siege the opportunity for a reformation
remains on the evil trail, to tear down the redeemed
the redeemed power of rejection continues to prevail
The persecutor suffers a harsh consequence
of harassment by another wicked soul
one who also refuses the many signals to turn around
another one who God will deal with on time
the redeemed, by withstanding the test of persecution
applies spiritual growth, consistent with peace at mind

Outer Reality Zone

Pray for those who are out of control
cannot face self not in tune with time
underneath the denial and false pretense
reality becomes too heavy on the mind
freedom cannot mean staying on the run
that has to be stressful pretending this is fun
too late to recapture the life that once was
yet efforts are not made for a brighter future
coming in contact with the undesirable
creating much more unnecessary trouble
no good can come from that way of life
Take care of yourself take my advice
stay sober to distinguish right from wrong
pray for those in need to find the strength
to rise up from the outer reality zone

What is Happiness?

Can happiness actually be sadness in denial
is happiness more significant living in luxury
can happiness exist living in the way of poverty
happiness is emotion only the soul of happiness knows
Can happiness exist with those who live in drama
can the happiness of one soul depend upon another
can happiness show up on the face of pain
only true happiness of a soul can truly explain
Does happiness come to an end when trouble begin
is happiness like a leaf that disappears and come again
is happiness a smile that sometime seem deceiving
happiness is expressed by the soul of happiness

The Door

I see Democracy as the Door
the door to liberty, respect, and courtesy
however one may rate economically
the door should remain accessible
The door to opportunity
whether a person should enter or not
the door should remain unlocked
The door to knowledge
for all children of all races
with all patterns of behavior
all deserving to be educated
the door should remain unlocked
The door to shelter
whether anyone should enter or not
the door should remain unlocked

A Longer Prayer

Seems like suddenly you are famous
and categorized as high profile
your creation is now in public view
critics will judge your personal affairs
as you face the media and the public
you are always to keep in memory of
the humbleness on the journey to success
driven passion was put to the test
determination is the key to your fame
the origin of your endeavor to honor
you are now sharing the craft with fans
this is an additional amazing blessing
to cherish each and every moment
to give thanks in a longer prayer
for a work of art special and rare

Life is Full of Life

Life is the reality based not upon a fantasy
life is full of life!...life is full of life!
life brings on the good times with calmness
days breezing right along with smoothness
and suddenly there are heartaches with a vengeance!
life then seems unfair by letting contentment down
waving through tides… but then, back onto the bridge!
risen up again and turned around!
There comes the time to wake up and see the light
with open eyes to see what life is really about
a living guide, has been established, to follow through
for choosing what's best; what truly counts
Life reveals not what tomorrow will bring
but today gives the right to follow potentials
to acknowledge the restless rhythm deep within
the desire to challenge the destination
the thirst for satisfaction for the good of existing
Life is the reality based not upon a fantasy
a journey leading to where?.. or when?
to face up to reality, at times it's good to pretend
life is the reality, based not upon a fantasy
life is full of life!...life is full of life!

Genuine

The thought process
of common sense
opens up a genuine world
of understanding
to discover the roots of a problem
intellectual sense
must turn to common sense
right from wrong
to turn confusion into resolve

Listen to God

God has something for you to say
it's okay, He will prepare you
something for you to do
with patience, He will see you through
Brace up with courage
confusion will come into play
make the move anyway
don't worry about your imperfections
He's more concerned about your intentions
listen, trust, and obey
Because your work stands for inspiration
your role requires no competition
how do I know?... an humble child as I?
I listened, and I heard Him say
"Trust Me, it will be okay!"

For the Sake of Humanity

Yesterday, men, women, the young, the old, came together
in a non-violent, yet activated spirit, of protesting injustice
and inequality, to desegregate society as the out-look
a challenge in harms way, the blue print laid out for today
one person at a time, a chain reaction, is what it took

Today, in the diverse demographics, time itself created
if only to treat one another, as we desire to be treated
in the eyes of God; to be intolerant of racial-hatred
publically defaming, someone's character, is no game
equality, caters not to percentage, *labored the majority*
or the minority, equality liberates people, of all backgrounds
including the poor child, facing complexity in life
equality gives the child the possibility to rise to the potential
by an adequate educational system, without a doubt
the preparation for achievements, rather than *hand outs*

Governmental Officials, please be led by common sense
policy making; not guerrilla warfare, but by compromise
with awareness that partisanship breeds obstruction
polarization can spread across the nation
In the final decision making, be in touch with the truth
it is alright to focus, on the right thing to do
true leadership brings things into the proper prospective
We the people of the United State, keep unity into action
democracy continues to blossom, by the work in progress
gathering fruits of the labor, the next generation will inherit

In Touch With the Children

Our children are the leaders of tomorrow
for now, they are the product of today
influenced by what we do, show, and what we say
children can become followers
but not necessarily by something good
we are the ones to set the good example
and give direction, as we should
In today's world of revolving technology
making connections amazingly swift
by face to face communication
we know who our children are with
the child is the product of who we are creating
Bring out the best of the child
and not the worst. We say it takes a village
but the village can't help very much
when the family is out of touch
youth can get caught up in media fantasy
a beautiful mind develops not by cosmetic surgery
self-esteem applies to confident behavior
a concerned parent, is the best motivator

Let Us Pray for the Children

Let us find a way to communicate
for some moments, set aside technology devices
look into the eyes of a child, the windows to the soul
feel the child's hunger to eliminate the inferiority
in America who boast of its democracy
lead our children into the comfort zone for learning
historical figures of yesterday had a yearning
for the next generation to follow footsteps of success
to climb above stumbling blocks of injustice
slowing down the progress of equality in society
Where is our compassion, do we have the heart
to bring our children out of the dark?
some children uphold a spirit of determination
to withstand the stress and continue on excelling
let us lift up the children whose spirits are broken
think of each and every child as a special token
encouragement is more effective than so much blame
and while we are striving to make a difference
let us remember to pray for the children

On the Way to Reality

Financial mismanagement from a national view
piles up irresponsibly, on the brink of disaster
Out of work, financial problems, causing dismay
some individuals handles the stressful days
with negative distractions to peace and harmony
It's a good time for applying a stronger faith
to start new beginnings with humbleness of spirit
With no money to create over materialistic clutter
it's a good time to get more in touch with reality
credit cards no longer hand things on a civil platter
less food on the plate, looses the extra weight
less money creates thrifty spending plans
the grocery bag becomes the liner for the trashcan
some individuals escape to the clouds in the sky
others spend hard-earned money on a sensible high
becomes the entrepreneur, whatever may apply
Face reality about the roots creation of recession
to make it right, fair, and civil, learn the lesson!

It's All About Me

If I should die and come back again
I would come back as me
of course I would do some things better
perfect on this earth, I could never be
as for success?
I would learn the same life lessons
or even more, never less
I would have no limits on education
as for spirituality on this earth
forever a work in progress
If I could not be me
with other choices… now let me see
what would I be?.. I would be a bird
perhaps a robin, flying free, adorned in red
seems like a pretty cool things to be
If my Lord has a plan, as to who I will be
that's certainly alright with me!

Seasoned

We of the world are vulnerable to sinfulness
at times I wonder why? Are You still there O Lord
to calm the unrest? I think about You, the Savior
on the cross of crucifixion, I know You are my fortress
At times my emotions get carried away
through a revolving door in my mind
I must persevere by the very same power, on the day
the Lord saw fit, to turn my life around
The reflections of my contentment is not spared
from antagonism, I must pray for alternatives
to avoid useless argument
reflections of my contentment, is at times misconstrued
I must never to ignore the spiritual instinct
when to speak, or when to keep my peace
when to embrace or when it is best to keep my space
love consumes my heart with no room for hate
As a spiritual warrior, the battle of life gets tough
I wonder why innocent children in the world
must suffer so much? Once again, You heard my cry
by amazing grace, use me, to enlighten a better place

To Go on Believing

The starlight of the nighttime
revolve into the dawning of sunlight
in the early morn
like magic it seems, like the passion
reaching the destination
Magnificent adventures emerge
the perfect time along the way
such as the journey of envisioning
and the reaping of the splendor

Harmoniously Speaking

Photographs

A pleasant mood is in the air, excitement riding high
the city is looking good, hosting the eventful occasion
appreciating and celebrating the liberty of our Nation
"Circle Line Pier 83.... I cruised on this boat before
This ice cream taste so good, I have to have some more!"
"Let's take a picture of the Statue of Liberty!"
Cruising past the Burroughs, bridges a few
getting the party started, with a lots more things to do
the young and young at heart is blending with the mix
the *"Big Apple"* is hosting this very special weekend 1986
South Street Seaport, on the walking tour
eleven blocks of vendors paradise, in business for sure
The beautiful Water Street Park at Pier 16 and 17
the *Historic Seaport District,* ships like you've never seen
we're eating out in the open air, getting full as a tick
basking in holiday glory... It's Liberty Weekend 1986
On the Fourth of July we are in Queens New York
visiting our relatives, having fun at the beach, cooking out
gracious hospitality, that's what it's all about
faintly thunderous fire works are sparkling the sky
colorful formations, exploding more beautifully lavish
"These are the unique moments, created to cherish!"

Grand-Ma's Pancakes

A child's world is spontaneous
and that's just fine
good enough to last a lifetime

"Grandma may I have
another pancake please?
your pancakes are the best
way better than Mommy's"

"Bless your little heart grandson
but don't tell your Mommy
I gave you a cup of coffee!"

Genuine Satisfaction

I made a ninja turtle costume
for my cute little grandson OJ
his neighborhood pals wanted one
he wore that cute costume
even to bed as well as to play
at times all day – he outgrew it
still he wore it like it was new
the ninja turtle costume wore out
OJ had worn it for years
his family with smiles, gladly said:
We're not shedding any tears!"

At Walt Disney World

No matter what age, it was all about fun, a fantastic game!
At Planet Hollywood, we dined like stars, with good food on the plate!
Sea World Show, was so incredible, just in time we were not too late!
Two grandsons and I enjoyed, the Beauty and the Beast show!
Aladdin's Royal Caravan, what a magical way to go!
Mickey Mania Parade, a mouse full of fun!
Splash Mountain got us all wet up, rapidly coming down in the sun!
Back to the Future Rocket Ride, went back in time a swirling!
approaching avalanches !.. dinosaurs!.. a volcano!
escaping through the Hill Valley!.. we went a whirling!
Little Mermaid Show, what a wonderful place to be!
we felt the magical ocean breeze, the sensational spray of the sea!
On the King Kong Ride, destruction was on the brink!
The Boat Ride was so smooth… then Jaws came on the attack!
escape to survival, called for a refreshing drink!
On the Fourth of July, the rain, put us on the run
luckily we had already taken the escapade, a splendid day of fun!
The five Day trip at Walt Disney World, with unity hand in hand
with fantasy fireworks in the sky, very well worth the plan!

Facing the Fear

Bike riding on the school campus ground
Stanley and Christian road several times around
At the stadium, Christian quickly got off the bike
"Come on Stanley, let's climb way up to the top!"
And off Christian went... to the top of the steps
then waved to Stanley... "Come on up ... real high!"
High step, Stanley did not like, and rather not try
So off he started to ride the bike... but lingered a while
wanting to join Christian, not wanting to be outdone
and besides, way up top, seemed like a lot of fun
Christian stood tall, hands straight towards the sky
His Mom scolded, from the family picnic near by
"Come down Christian... Make this your last time!"
Christian didn't seem to pay his mom no mind
Loudly, he urged Stanley, "Come on up to see far!"
acting like he was a brave little superstar
Off the bike, without a cease, on top of the steps
was Stanley, with a big grin, like he did it with ease!
The crowd, with surprise, applauded and cheered
"Christian helped Stanley to face up to his fear!"
"and Stanley took the risk without shedding a tear!"
Down the steps... on the bikes... riding away
seven years old cousins became heroes at play!

The Richness of Family

On this family reunion, together we salute
a very special celebration, for me and for you
we are including our ancestors from back in the years
on this occasion, we may shed joyful tears...
Long ago, a foundation was laid, by the price of survival
our ancestors paid. From a personal point of view
we are thinking of love ones not here
this is all about our heritage, applying to me and to you
Where would we be without the richness of family
inherited from the past, and presently meant to last?
The creative patterns of survival by our ancestors
contributed to American folklore, of a worldwide nature
I can see the glow on Daddy's face...
carving on a puppet doll, his most relaxing thing to do...
reweaving the old rocking chair like new...
blowing a tune on the harmonica...beating his drum
...picking a tune on the guitar strings...
finally I can hear Daddy say: *I'm passing on this creativity*
to my offspring to use in a different way
The quilt Ma put together, spoke a language of its own
hand sewn, colorful scrap cloth, never to grow cold
Waves, are a part of the sea, seagulls along the shore
separated from the team, yet follows the scheme of unity
the main source that reigns, together we salute
the richness of family, may forever remain the same!

Humor for Seasoning

When stress is boiling over
to calm down the overflowing
stir in a little humor for seasoning
when difficulty is seriously brewing
just a few sprinkles of laughter
simmers down the tension
makes a big difference in the texture
add a little nonsense to the seriousness
handling the business gets easier
to more balmy and less bitter
the taste of confusion gets better
for life conditioning and reasoning
add a little humor for seasoning

Colors of Springtime

Bright sunshine is glowing
on a dazzling array of colors, geraniums
tulips, azaleas, and daffodils
neatly shaven green grass covers the ground
Underneath the shade of dogwood trees
baring white blossoms
crowds are strolling along the walkway
blending a sound of well being
cool breeze is waltzing
by *Mother Natures'* free and perfect show
a wondrously picnic way to go!"

Materialistic v. the Friendliness in Me

I was walking on a tour of my neighboring community
the day was pleasant, individuals, passing by me, were not
"walker friendly?" I didn't think so…at least not towards me
no eye contact, no smiles, not even a *"How Do You Do?"*
"I should've worn my bright red blouse with lace!"
Another day, I got a smile, by the *"Good Morning Ma-am"*
I felt a nice vibe…
"Is this because of the appearance change I made?...yes it is I'm afraid"
my red lipstick matched my bright red blouse with lace
finger nails freshly done; ponytail neatly in place
eyebrows arched evenly, easy spirit snickers nice and clean
I was looking classy, in good fitting jeans!
individuals walking pass me, were obviously impressed
All I needed from the beginning, was to exchange greetings
not according to my style of dress, but by my friendliness
the friendliness in me, comes quite naturally

Cool

Dancing and singing hilariously
pretending to be a cool star
he is the seven years old idol
of his one fan, stuffed Teddy Bear
making moves all over the place
the wild dance he's doing
now in the living room...oops!
the potted plant is ruined

The Deli Routine

Busy at work in the deli department
the rule of courtesy is in mind
"We do not let the customers wait
Fooling around is a waste of time!"
The cook sure know how
to cook chicken in the deep fry
crispy brown, finger licking good
enticing for customers to buy
Wipe down the cases
fill up meats and cheese
salads are due, by assignment
no later, if you please
Happy Birthday on cake orders
goes as the customers desire
Stop that phone from ringing
right now!
Stock the shelves, pastries, bread
party trays, due today and days away
fruits trays… please make
avoid those customers complaints!
"Much more goes on
in this work zone, major cleaning up
a little fun, a little play
a little groaning, to handle the day
as for boredom – not any – no way
"It's pay day, you bet!"
"Please may I have my pay check?"

Parenting Rap

"*G*et out of the bed right now, get washed up"
"get ready for school on time, don't miss the bus!"
Kids are pretending not to wake up
even by the sound of Mom's serious voice
Next on the program, early morning chaos!
In the evening after dinner, kids are having fun
the laughter turns into pushing and shoving
"Just shove it back where it came from"
"Run the water for bathing, not splashing"
"one at a time…nothing changed… make it soon"
"Wrong way…that way is the bathroom!"
" Take a look at these school notices, Honey"
"Are we suppose to be made out of money?"
"the field trip, calling for a hundred dollars"
"the fund donations due, as soon as tomorrow"
"No! you can't have a bed time snack!"
"Look at you, dripping water all over, the place!"
"Stop the drama! Did the reading get read?"
At last!... parents have sighed and said
"The only sweet four kids is when asleep in bed!"

Language of its Own

A literary performance
appears on the stage of the soul
liberating the mind
authenticity of freedom of speech
a compilation of sentiments
reflections of yesterday's happenings
today and tomorrow
not so appealing to everyone
not sounding exactly right
at times metaphorically speaking
the art of making a point
whether appreciated – or not
to those who could care less
poetry speaks love and respect

Food

The cook, as usual brings to mind
what to cook for dinner on time
she goes stirring, and tasting
adding seasoning, and basting
pleasing expressions are on faces
pleasant aroma, all over the place
the cook is willing and smart
treats food, like a work of art
everyone's ready for a taste
warmed up leftovers, not to waste

Skateboard Super Star

The skateboard superstar is my grandson
been skating since the age of seven
zooming!... leaping!... whirling all around!
all at the same time!
taking on a rhythm coming down!
this is his passion, a sense of freedom
his Mom and Dad have trembled
through the ups!...downs!... tumbles around!
zooming in the air!...back on land!
the skateboard superstar
my grandson, is now a young man

Imaginary Miss Elliot

She's dignified and citified
to lively music, she dances
a little on the funny side
her not so funny jokes are hilarious
in a flowing dress of rainbow colors
she refuse to go unnoticed
she sings deliberately off key
the life of the party
this lady has freedom of expression
absolutely pleasing to have around
with a gorgeous smile
she's unique, her spirit is alive
she's one vivacious lady

Greetings

Say good morning it's ok
also say good afternoon
speak to people you know
make a good impression
Say nice things to people
throughout the work place
spread joy distinctively
find the time, create space
Shake a hand in church
hug loved ones at home
give a positive image
greetings sets the tone
Show your love anytime
to someone not as nice
to put up with coldness
friendliness cuts the ice

Hair Decisions

It's time for a different hairstyle
create a new look, like a movie star
be original, start a fresh new trend
make people stare, impress a few
Add color, curls, or wear it straight
such a personal choice to make
skinny braids, or cornrows, or a wig
or a relaxer, with lengthy extensions
What about a short cut, neatly trimmed
each style, an eye catching creation
why not let it grow, a big afro?
the natural beautiful way to go
work it to a level of satisfaction
All of those suggestions are fabulous
an eye catching creation
this low maintenance ponytail
is working okay, at least for another day

Some Folks are so Creative

What makes some folk so creative
is it a gift within the soul
what makes an interest turn to gold?
Some folk dress very well
with good taste on display
is it more about the time they gave?
Does it take born creativity
to decorate a house, or a brilliant mind
to write an outstanding book?
Does taste buds ability
create wonderful things to cook?
Some folk are such amazing parents
mother wit or father wit they say
Some folk are legendary good actors
the genes seem to be at play
The athletes' game goes strong
the opponents' game goes terribly wrong
What makes some folk so creative?
It comes from nothing but the truth
personal talent from deep within
comes out for others to approve

Charming

Your face is round
your eyes are sparkling
yours cheeks are soft
you are special
in your eyelet dress with lace
you are a dream
when I am blue
I look at you
you put a smile on my face

Adoring Rain

I like the rain!
the air is getting a cleansing
a walk in the rain is refreshing
often rain is referred to as pain
the garden will not complain
rain will change its tempo
from one rhythm to another
flowing down on the seasons
no preference for one or the other
crystal clear energy glistens
moments to relax and listen
rain at times is seen as a bother
restless with authority
pouring down, taking its space
moving at a widespread pace
suppressing the sunshine for days
a drought will not complain
"I like the rain!"

Home

Home is the place that shows the way
to turn to through the restless days
the holder of the love showing up on faces
as for animosity, a loving home has no space
At a time of home at the amusement park
the older ones hang out with the young ones
Through the holiday season
there is no better place to be to share gifts
with the warmth of family
The place with stories of old school value
pictures of special occasions, laughter, the tears
where ever one may roam
the faith to carry on into the years
rich, poor, huge, small, when love surrounds
it's nice to go back home

Autumn

Mother Nature's magical skills
appears on the leaves in blazing colors
golden, maroon, shades of red and orange
rust, yellow, and olive green
she dresses up an abundance of trees
the artistic environment is "pretty cool"
the time to refresh and renew
to anticipate celebrations
and many wondrous things to do
falling leaves on the ground, is ok by me
"I like the Autumn season!"

Timeless Music

Kindness is warm
like sunshine on a Winters day
kindness is comforting
like pain eased away
kindness is lyrical
like a humming bird sings
kindness is peaceful
kindness is a smile
no one can tear apart
kindness comes from a place
deep within the heart
the world becomes a better place
by kindness along the way
profoundly authentic
a timeless kind of music

Uptown Queen City

Dominant huge cooperate buildings, are towering
outdated residential areas are long gone and upgraded
the lavish Convention Center host affairs of galaxy
Charlotte, the queen city on the rise, is highly innovated
Contemporary models of museums, theaters, art centers
educational facilities, hotels, condos are all over the place
The church of historical value, of expertise construction
Is still standing out beautifully, in the original space
The Epicentre is a lo-cal of restaurants, a movie theater
places of business, banking convenience, a retail shop
young adults are patrons at quite a few night spots
Appetizing aroma flows the air from fancy restaurants
youngsters are skateboarding, all mixed in with pedestrians
dog walkers, runners, bikers, traffic is steadily moving
In Time Warner Cable Arena, basketball fans are cheering
the hometown team, owned by the legendary Michael Jordan
Bank of America Stadium is packed with football fans
huge crowds are drawn to the festivals in the street
Nascar Hall of Fame Museum, holds great attractions
Taxicabs are catering to visitors, a growing population
Light Rail, commutes to and from work places
Massive transportation is *a must* – in future making
Luxurious residential areas, typical for professionals
with brief cases, walking to convenient work places
seeming not to see, the homeless in the street, not very far
Uptown Queen City has her sight on reaching the star

Relationship Anew

We got through the emotional experience
spoiling our friendship, a matter of difference
we are back to speaking from the heart
we will be friends through thick and thin
our relationship will not become torn apart
Angry words were getting the best of us
taking control to the point of disgust
now unnecessary to even mention
because it made more sense to realize
a relationship, is worth more than an argument
Together we brought about forgiveness
problems are corrected, we are connected
our relationship is intact and anew
confusion has finally left us alone
"thumbs-up!... we have our friendship to rely on!"

Rhythm of Africa

I heard many times about the continent of Africa
the television screen, too often show
nothing more than images of conflictive poverty
but what do I know of this land of my ancestry?
Ancient Africa, soul of grandeur, centuries ago
empires, great kings and queen... what do I know?
O but to be among the Africans
the herds of giraffes, elephants, the souring eagles
to listen to the stringed instruments, the harp
the drum, to wear the kente cloth with the people
to learn about the tribes my ancestor stemmed from
to be touched by undying hope of Nelson Mandela
and the wise disciplined Arch Bishop Tu Tu
About the rich land of Africa of sun blistering gold
my heart knows only the rhythm within my soul

A Medley of Poem

A poetic convention was held at a lavish hotel
a friendly atmosphere, of poets and their guest
as travelers from afar and near
Readings went on by poets of different age groups
from different walks of life
participants in poetry bashes, workshops, lectures
The banquet was terrific, by romantic classics
The reception providing a soft piano sound
dancers graced the stage a second time around
The Awards Ceremony, contestants on pins to win!
the finalist of different walks of life
of different age groups lined the stage!
And the winner claimed the grand prize!
all attending poets shared something in common
a poetical occasion, especially to rise!

Universal Harmony

How fascinating, the world never runs out of song
enough for the world to sing along
young sound especially for rocking and rolling
rhythm and blues, soul music, ballads for listening
the parade steps on time with the marching band
moving by the sound of drum beats and fans
a vibrant tune for late afternoon, the guitar strings
for romancing and slow dancing, the horn vibrato
organ music works miracles for the church choir
beautiful opera, a truly musical blending of art
country music sounds are upbeat, slow, or sweet
a musical form of poetry the tom – toms of Africa
the bagpipe, the harp, the whistling tunes are personal
the classic symphony of the classic orchestra
blending instruments, a dynamic jazz rhythm
rap sounds off by drum beats and exotic dancers
All music in its own good sound is beautiful
Universal harmony, enough to sing along
How fascinating the world never runs out of song!

Happy New Year!

Happy New Year! I'm glad to be hear
get up off your feet and dance to the beat
give a wave to the past, make a great wish
that good times will last, celebrate the presence
the past has generously sent the joy all around
It's time to make a new start, a new you
keep up the cheer, I'm glad to still be here
say it loud and clear! Happy New Year!

Seasonal Love on Valentines Day

The glow of our love warms a frosty morn
days of ice covered trees, a spectacular land
beaming faces are covered with snowflakes
the feeling is hilarious, mischievously grand
Romance like ours is special and cozy
listening to the soothing whispers of the wind
our hearts beat in rhythm with the calm rain
falling pitter-patter against the window pain
As we are strolling along in a gentle bond
a performance graces the scenery by the pond
the humming birds melodies are quite a wonder
butterflies goes waltzing from plant to flower
Our affair is just as solid as the tall mountain
and wonderful – and free like the robin flying
in the chilly breeze, mingling gently in the trees
the ground is glazed with multicolor leaves
This is the day with the bright sunshine
the night with the moon and the stars above
because you and I blend compatible together
each season blends well with our love

Easter

Jesus Christ the Lord and Savior
suffered the crucifixion
and endured the resurrection
Give thanks, give praise
to the Savior, the King
the power for repentance
the amazing grace for redemption

O Lord hold my hand
I am a child of youth
guide me into Your wisdom
to live by Your truth

And by this blessing, I am used
to let my little light shine
as encouraging to others
as we abide upon this earth
may we give thanks, give praise
to the Savior, the Holy Birth

A Broadway Play for Mothers Day

Among the clouds we were on the way
the airplane landed on time on a perfect day
first on the program, I got a foot massage
the pedicure made me feel high on a pedestal
As a *Queen* for a couple of days in *NY City*
dressed casual but looking trendy and pretty
the trip to *New York* on this special occasion
The Color Purple, was the main attraction
among the participants waiting in the long line
we entered the *Broadway Theater* on time
Walking, taking a taxi, leisurely getting around
taking photographs of sights here and about
in stores shopping, eating not to be left out
meeting up with relatives at a cozy restaurant
food was delicious, the tea was nice and hot
This *Mothers Day Gift*, a major appreciation
last on the program, breakfast at the lavish hotel
simple moments, extremely sentimental
especially the famous *Broadway Play*
two loving daughters, made me a *Queen*
at least for a couple of days

Memorial Day

On Memorial Day
the American way
we pay tribute to fallen soldiers
in battle of massive
lost of lives
for the freedom of humanity
on Memorial Day
the American way
we pay tribute
to the fallen soldiers
we place a flower on a grave

Celebrating Dad

Dad is the ideal provider
he makes us well aware, of responsibilities
"Living is not always free, not always leisure play!"
then willingly hand us money and playfully say
"You guys get to stepping, out'a my way!"
His same song is: *"Someday son, you'll walk in my shoes"*
as for education it's: *Either you will win, or lose!*
we do our chores without *too much* fooling around
Dad will compliment: *"This is fine!"*
On weekends off with us, Dad spends quality time
those two lovebirds call Mom and Dad
their actions speaks much louder than words
yet the two, can get on each other's *last nerve*
actually Mom is the boss, usually she has the final say
"Dad deserve *some slack,* it's Fathers Day!"
It's, clear to see the family unity

The Fourth of July

We are celebrating, the birth of the Nation
with barbeque chicken, on the grill
the fish is seasoned to fry!

We have a good spot, in the crowd at the park
a traditional gathering, our favorite place
fireworks are *the bomb* in your face!

The Fourth of July, the spectacular way to say
the Declaration of Independence
"value freedom in the USA!"

Labor Day

Celebrate the privilege
of having a job
it's time to take off to go play
we can go to the parade
and take in a sports event
just live it up, dine out
money earned is money spent
we will celebrate Labor Day
and not worry about the cash
we will set aside the bills
why not enjoy the stash
let's go on a shopping spree
another pay check want be long
today we will celebrate
'til money will be all gone

Grandmother Deserve a Celebration

Grandmother is not to be underrated
she truly deserve to be celebrated
always handling her emotions with prayer
insisting that her children be well aware
she is still the ruler of sternness and care
faith shows through her everyday living
noble, a reflection of love and devotion
she is the holder of the ties that bind
the expert at hugging and drying eyes
her wisdom is not to be underrated
Grandmother deserve to be celebrated

One Day of Halloween

Set aside reality, join in the fun land
of fantasy, just show up at a door
but make sure it's someone you know
you're a monster, and I'm a witch
let's crash the crazy party
let's fit in, with the wild and the rowdy
who can be boring, it's Halloween
funny looking freaks, make a welcome scene
it's all over, life goes on
the reality way, cannot be a fantasy
for more than a day
dressed in all kinds of hilarious stuff
one day of Halloween is enough

Veterans Day

This American holiday
especially for the Veterans
who went to war
for the sake of freedom
for humanity
at battle at any cost
we celebrate
and for peace we pray
remembering to set aside this day
to honor the Veterans

This Thanksgiving Day Prayer

Nature's colors tones the day
the family gathering is warm
home cooked food is plentiful
Thanksgiving Day is special
like the visiting Autumn season
holiday guest fade away
Thanksgiving may take its place
in hearts and minds to stay
as we set aside this special day
to acknowledge our blessings
we are reminded to leave behind
unnecessary complaining
But to count blessings each day
and think about those in need
of health and strength to succeed
we pray for love ones not here
as a special part of us so dear
This prayer as a daily curriculum
we pray to do good deeds
and leave selfishness behind
we pray to do our very best
we give thanks all of the time

Christmas Season Images

The Star
shines above
the Christmas tree
folks are making a list
that seems to have no end
busy at Christmas shopping
having a few parties to attend
beautiful decorations on the tree
with lights and colorful ornaments
around the tree are loads of presents
falling snow enhances the atmosphere
to be true to tradition is to bask in cheer
all things are achieved and now in place
a trip to the grocers put an end to the haste
preparations, worth the effort, worth the magic
observing the season can become quite hectic
family gathers for dinner with music traditionally
for some, Jesus Christ birth is observed spiritually
on this Christmas occasion family shares the love
Jesus Christ has a gift to offer
one of a very miraculous kind
especially to be yours and mines
His gift of grace is for all times

Let Us Celebrate Kwanzaa

The African America celebration of ancestry
based on unity, determination
responsibility, cooperation in economics
purpose, faith, creativity
Kwanzaa is celebrated
with symbolic objects
reflecting modern traditional concepts
fruits and vegetables
a place matt
the candleholder with seven candles
ears of corn
symbolizing the children in the home
the communal cup
seven principals in large print
hung high to observe
fundamental principles, a guide for living

Traditional Time Out

It's time to go and have some fun
It's well before dark
off we go to the amusement park!
Kids go on the water ride
to slide on down really fast is so cool
while grownups are relaxing
kids take off to splash in the pool!
The explosive Top Gun Ride!
kids are being shot straight up!
quickly unbuckling and hurrying off
"It wasn't scary that much!"
In the spooky haunted house
there's a real live mummy!
now for the really refreshing stuff
a fruity slushy is yummy
It's times to get on the way
what a very special place for fun!
enjoying a family time out
that's what I'm talkin' 'bout!

An Earthly Reminder

An array of beautiful crepe myrtle trees
beneath the sky of clattering thunder
suddenly subsides
sprinkles of rain, amid the rolling clouds
refreshes the air
flocks of birds are spreading wings
night time is romancing
the moon and the stars, softly shining bright
earthly abundance enough to share
enough to suit the taste
to treat the earth better is mindful not to waste
the earth bares its great hurdles
my favorite tree blossoms
in early Springtime, the crepe myrtle

A Dance in Basketball Rhythm

The players are in rhythm on court
defender challenging the offender
overpowering strong aggression!
rising above the adversity... a shot on target!
Roles are in reverse
a dance one on one becomes a miss
but not without another chance
a rhythm in, a rhythm out, with fierceness!
capturing the rim with a vengeance!
Last chance, last dance, a goal is defeated!
with disappointed demeanors
the winners eyes are gleaming
by outsmarting, rebounding, defending
A dance in rhythm with a basket ball
performs the dance of living

Jewel

My jewel was hidden away
many times I touched the jewel
touched by the glow, until one day
I removed the jewel from the hiding place
what good is a hidden jewel
when the value can only mean
the glow so bright is meant to be seen
Into the reflection of innocent years
happiness, loneliness, tears
anxiety to claim individuality
the mirror of experiences, evolves with
the developing of maturity
Many a moment in life is spent
trying to figure things out, like placing art
above an aged piece of furniture
to enrich the historical value
to enhance the expertise craft
What matters the most for a life time
… genuine love and laughter…
the value can only mean
the glow so bright is meant to be seen

A Noteworthy Living Experience

The Creative Sayings of African Americans

(a poetic essay)

The Sayings of African Americans, it's old... it's young... it's hip... it's bold. I've lived it, and loved the *trends* all my life, quite frankly, it's because I'm black! It's speech folk lore, rooted in the dialect of the Plantation Negro. Not out of ignorance, as some may say... *here's the thing...* When the African came to America, his native tongue – his language was stripped away. His identity was transplanted and became the American slave – nothing more. An educated slave?... was totally unheard of. By the cravings for freedom and independence, the need to communicate among themselves, slaves listened and picked up on the meaning of words being spoken, within the plantation environment, yet to mimic those who oppressed them – they were reluctant. Instinctively among themselves the plantation Negro (regional speech pattern) dialect developed. The dialect accepted in the poetry of Paul Laurence Dunbar . By the time of the Harlem Renaissance, the jazz era (in the 1920's) the dialect in the poetry of Langston Hughes was upgraded.

*Slang...Ebonics...Black English...Spoken Soul...*It's the rich inheritance of African American speech folklore: communication, identity, ethnic pride, and independence.

The Latest Saying, adds a touch of life to the English language. Some *Sayings* can be unfavorable but that's human nature. Unfavorable speaking goes on in all languages, in all nations, in all races – of all kinds.

Some people of the races speak the *Sayings* of the African American. It's passionate, *Whassup?..* it's cool, it's rhythms and rhymes. I've lived it – and loved trendy *Sayings* all my life. We *keep it real,* we keep it clean, cause it's *da bomb!* It's so American! It's unity among us – it's fun and free. *Trust me!* – African Americans claims ownership of the trendy originations, yet do not claim it as a substitute for standard English language. Most African Americans speak English well – like we should. So *get with the program!... It's all good!*

The Enduring Life of the Negro

(a poetic essay)

The Sharecropper: Sews the seeds and fertilizes the soil, producing bounteously for the prosperity of society, except for the life of the sharecropper...

The Common Laborer: His industrial job revolve up and down like the range of restless waves of the sea. So does the mood swings of the Laborer, with the heavy weight of the wind against his shoulders, in need of the shift to a lighter breeze...

The Musically Creative Negro: Desiring to be like the song bird, adding melody to the world, flying above mountains, crossing over the plains and forest. In reality the oppressor's intensive work load, holds down the dream of the Musically Creative Negro, whose trusting in God's plan, and releases the emotional stress and strain in a soulful song and dance rhythm on stage. His natural rhythms are like the song bird influencing personalities from different nationalities – personalities who imitate the Negro's creation and with *a majority fan base* succeeds the fortune and fame of the Negro's *minority fan base*...The fate of The Musically Creative Negro, seems *cannot win for losing...*

The Achiever: With a brilliant knowledge applying to educating and uplifting the Negro people, the humble, the weak the strong willed, children, elders, the good willed, the God fearing. The Achiever, gives back to society, yet cannot fulfill the desires to uplift all of the Negro people – especially those whose lives are diminishing deeper in poverty. The odds are as greatly stacked against The Achiever, as the rest of the Negros, whatever the roll in society, yet The Achiever rises to a better quality of life by an amazing strength of endurance...

The Civil Rights Worker: Tackles the wild weeds of injustice, sews seeds of human dignity for the sake of elevating the status of the Negro in society and the labor is handed over to the life of the African American.

Culturally Unique Soul Expressions

(a poetic essay)

African Americans have upheld the desire to establish a distinctive identity remaining true to heritage. The Civil Rights Movement of the 1950's and 60's gained equality for African Americans as well as a renewed sense of identity. The identity as Negros or colored people evolved as African American, with a renewed sense of proud, influenced by the legendary singer James Brown, *Say it Loud I'm Black and I'm Proud.*

The African American southern folklore – styles of clothing and adornment, cooking (down home style) arts and crafts, poetry, music, song, dance and *creative sayings,* traditionally tells the story of black American experiences, including struggles – as a people uprooted from the African origin and transplanted into America.

One of the many oppressive rules for the enslaved was a restriction from learning to read or become educated. The slaves who attended the white man's church services, observed the reading of certain Scriptures as relevant to their suffering ~ to their longing to be free from servitude, yet they could not expect that to happen during their life time. Slaves working in the fields, formed Words of Scripture into songs as a reflection of holding onto faith in God, to deliver their souls into heaven, the final resting place

Swing Low Sweet Chariot
Coming for to Carry Me Home

Through the passing of time, following the Emancipation (1865) freed slaves eventually formed their own places of worship and prayerfully sang hymns.

Go down Moses way down in Egypt land
Tell ol' Pharaoh to let my people go

Spiritual and gospel songs were sung with an intense hallelujah praise to God – bodies swaying, hand clapping, dancing, shouting by the drum beats and the rhythm of the music including the tambourine – performing a resilient approach to an oppressive way of survival, with faith in God as the power for deliverance from sin into redemption and rejuvenation

I went down to the valley to pray
My soul got happy and stayed all day

African American music and speech folklore *Develops as Trends and Popularizes Itself to the World.* Today in music as well as in other forms of mass popular culture, African Americans are much more influential than ever, directed towards widening the Nation's perception and understanding of African American values. Performers around the world, capitalize careers under the influence of African American *Culturally Unique Soul Expressions ~ folklore music, poetry, song and dance.*

Rock and Roll v. the Civil Rights Movement

(a short story)

The new upbeat sound played on the radio by black disk jockeys, "Maebelline" had reached the young black radio audience as an instant hit, *a more lively kind of the blues* recorded by a young black singer, writer, guitarist from Missouri name Chuck Berry, and the tone was set for "Rock and Roll Music." This new upbeat music was particularly favorable, first among black youth, and integrated also favorable to young white listeners…

At the "Do-Drop-In," located on the outskirts of the town of Wilson, were a crowd of young people. The place was under adult male supervision, and the rule for the *teenage bobby sockers* was: "No under age drinking alcoholic beverage" and a reasonable curfew to head for home. The only thing allowed was good clean fun. In those days boys practiced chivalry; held doors for girls as a courtesy; pursued girls, initiated the flirting and politely asked a girl for a dance. Willamena was an exception to the rule of flirting. This high school teenager usually took to the floor dancing all by herself, teasing the boys, she knew how to get the party started. The floor became crowded with partners. We young people loved Chuck Berry's music sounding on the *juke box* his style of expressing the complexity of young love interest in a rather wacky fun kind of lyrics – typical for letting loose and dance the *jitter-bug* to.

Tim danced with me to the romantic sound of the Drifters. Tim was one of the most popular and handsome boys in high school, his flirtation with me as we danced was simply intriguing. A gentleman obviously high – *on high school fame and popularity.*

I joined my best friend, Maebell and said to her, "Why do we fall for the most cutest and popular boy of them all? We don't stand a chance." Maebell was head over hill in love with Freddy, another cute popular boy. "Speak for yourself!" she said, and we fell out laughing!

Teenagers, naturally fun loving as themselves deserving to be, the music was an escape mechanism from the discontentment seriously brewing through conversations among grown folks, about having to face the same injustice their ancestors had faced; if nothing would be done to stop it, the next generation would be its next victims. In justice for black folk in America had reached the point of boiling over.

Little Richard came out with *Good Golly Miss Molly,* and his hits kept on coming. Author Grudup came out with *That's Alright Mama.* A female by the name of Willie Mae Big Mama Thornton, had made *Hound Dog* a hit *in (1952).* The music magnetized from one artist to the other, Elvis Presley, Bo Diddley, Fats Domino, Frankie Lyman and more. Rock and Roll was replacing the romantic do-wop music, but the do-wop music was so popular, would hang around for years to come before becoming *old school classics.*

Chuck Berry songs would include *Roll Over Bethoven (1956) Rock and Roll Music (1957) Sweet Little Sixteen and Johnny B. Good (1958).*

Little Richard became a consistent performer of his signature style of singing and rocking explosively at the piano. Through the years, Richard stuck to his original, *old school rock and roll,* as well as the hair do, the *pom-pa-dour,* all rock and roll. Richard would proclaim himself: *the Architect of Rock and Roll.*

As the Civil Rights Movement was organizing, Rock and Roll had a message for the souls of black youth, before entering into an overwhelming tumultuous period of time – to transform the American Society: *keep on dancing, while keeping hope and prayers alive!* And young black America did just that, *listening to the fabulous Motown sounds!*

The American Creed

By William Tyler Page

(A reminder of the belief)

I believe In the United States of America as a government
of the people, by the people, for the people; whose just
powers are derived from the consent of the governed; a democracy
in a Republic; a sovereign Nation of many sovereign States;
a perfect union, one and separable; established upon those
principles of freedom, equality, justice and humanity for which
American patriots sacrificed their lives and fortune.
I therefore believe it is my duty to my country to love it;
to support its constitution; to obey its laws; to respect its flag;
and to defend it against all enemies.

Frederick Douglass 1818 - 1895

a powerful pioneer for human rights

Frederick Baily was born in Maryland on a plantation
at the age of twenty, he was sick of the brutal treatment
the inhuman lack of consciousness of quilt by his master
the act of slavery on human beings was a disaster
He escaped to the North, no longer in the bondage of shame
learned to read and write, and Douglass became his last name
a brilliant speaker, the leader of the abolitionist movement
for the civil rights of slaves, formed decades before the Civil War
He was invited by the American Anti Slavery Society
to embark on a lecture tour, thus became recognized
as one of America's first great spokesman, at a troubled time
He served as an advisor to Abraham Lincoln during the Civil War
and published an influential antislavery paper, The North Star
He fought for the adoption of Constitutional Amendment
to guarantee voting privileges and civil liberties
with commitment, he courageously challenged the flight
published his autobiography in (1845) and won world wide fame
Frederick Douglass was a powerful voice for human rights
A living experience as always a work to consider in progress

A Tribute to Rosa Parks 1913 - 2005

a legendary figure for American Democracy
(12-1-1955)

Mrs. Rosa Parks, a Montgomery Alabama native
stepped aboard a city bus after a long day of working
she took a seat in the beginning area in the Negro section
A white man got on board and all of the seats had been taken
Rosa was ordered by the driver to give up her seat to the white man
the forty-two years old seamstress silently defended her character
tired of the degradation, she would not give up her seat
The driver called the police and Rosa Parks was arrested
and the incident was immediately publicized through the nation
the black community, as a chain reaction came together
groups of all levels got involved to organize a bus boycott
with the Rev. Martin King Jr. as the director
chosen because of his firm and outspoken spiritual conviction
Thus, became the origin of the Civil Rights Movement
the beginning of a perilous plight for equal rights
and racism against black Americans was exposed to the world
As the episodes continued to unfold on television
I was *18 years old* and watched in humiliation:
Segregationist harassing the boycotters walking to work
the police handcuffing Rev. Martin Luther King, was startling
yet, deep inside, I felt a sense of proud for the boycotters
refusing to deny themselves their constitutional rights
the suffering was for justice and liberty – for my freedom
from the shackles that bind as an everyday experience
The very courage, special and warm spirited Rosa Parks
was tired and fed up with injustice
she sat down for the sake of her dignity and freedom
yet became a legendary figure for American Democracy
and the world would remember her name.
On November 13, 1956, the United States Supreme Court,
affirmed a decision of a three-judge U.S.
District, declaring segregation on buses unconstitutional!

John F. Kennedy Addresses the Nation

John F. Kennedy 1917-1963

the 35th President of the United States 1960-63

Anti-Segregation demonstrations were going on across the south. Negros were demanding the justice and liberty for ALL – way past time due for them. The jailing of public protesters and their refusal to pay the fines, created a chain reaction of a jail-in movement; voter registration drives, sit-ins, massive marches, prayer demonstrations. Bus loads of Freedom Riders including white allies were crisscrossing the south. The demonstrators were severely harassed by white supremacist, and police brutality. Black sharecroppers were being evicted from their farms. It was the year of (1963) and black Americans saw no reason to celebrate the centennial of Emancipation Proclamation (1863) the promise had not yet to be fulfilled and they nonviolently demonstrated this fact in the street, up against the unyielding face of racism - televised before the eyes of the public. They faced police brutality and the irony of teeth clutching canine police dogs. They were prostrated with high pressured water hose; clubbed, bombed, tear gassed, kicked, stoned, spat upon, and murdered – as a results, the shameful images in a supposedly free society were exposed to the world. Two black students could not register for summer classes at the University of Alabama as was due. President Kennedy outmaneuvered the Alabama white supremacist Governor, George Wallace and forced the registration of the students at the University with the safety of federal troops. The President, highly affected by the moral crisis with growing tragedies, under his administration was compelled to make the case to white America for black equality…

On June 11, 1963, the eve of the centennial, President Kennedy delivered a nationally televised address, outlining his proposal for legislation baring segregation.

"The Negro baby born in American today," he said, "regardless of the section of the nation in which he is born, has about one-half as much chance of completing college, one-third as much chance of becoming a professional man, twice as much chance of earning $10,000 a year, a life expectancy which is seven years shorter, and the prospects of earning only half as much"

"This is not a sectional issue – nor is it a partisan issue. This is not even a legal or legislative issue alone. It is better to settle these matters in the courts than on the streets, and new laws are needed at every level, but law alone cannot make men right."

"We are confronted primarily with a moral issue. It is as old as the Scriptures and is as clear as the American Constitution. The heart of the question is whether all Americans are to be afforded equal rights and equal opportunities, whether we are going to treat our fellow Americans, as we want to be treated. If an American, because his skin is dark, cannot eat lunch in a restaurant open to the public; if he cannot send his children to the best public school available, if he cannot vote for the public officials who will represent him, if, in short, he cannot enjoy the full and free lives which all of us want, then who among us would be content to have the color of his skin changed and stand in his place? Who among us would then be content with the counsel of patience and delay?"

I wondered, "will Kennedy's speech affect his popularity... Will the white supremacist take his words as a threat... by standing up for civil rights, will Kennedy regret?"

"And when Americans are sent to Vietnam or West Berlin, we do not ask for whites only. It ought to be possible, therefore, for American students of any color to attend any public institution they select without having to be backed up by troops."

The President's civil rights proposal for the upcoming week, he said, "would include legislation that would force public accommodation – "hotels, restaurants, theaters, retail stores, and similar establishments" – to serve all customers, regardless of the race. This, he conceded, "seems to be an elementary right. Its denial is arbitrary indignity that an American in 1963 should have to endure, but many do." He also pledged that the federal government would become more aggressive in ending school segregation, noting that the pace of desegregation since the Supreme Court's *Brown v. Board of Education* ruling was "very slow."

"We cannot say to 10 percent of the population...that your children cannot have the chance to develop whatever talents they have; that the only way that they are going to get their rights is to go into the streets and demonstrate. I think we owe them, and we owe them ourselves a better country than that."

Hours after Kennedy's speech, a white supremacist shot Medger Evers in the back, a World War Two Veteran, one of Mississippi most influential civil rights leaders; his three children and wife watched helplessly as he lay in a pool of blood on the steps of their home In Jackson...And on the eve of Medgar Evers assassination, President Kennedy made a fourteen-and a half minute speech to the nation...

"One hundred years of delay have passed, the President said, since President Lincoln freed the slaves, yet their heirs, their grandsons are not fully free. They are not yet free from the bonds of injustice; they are not yet free from social and economic oppression. And this nation for its hopes and all its boast can not be fully free until all its citizens are free."

"We preach freedom around the world and we mean it. And we cherish our freedom here at home. But are we to say to the world – and much more importantly to each other – that this is the land of the free, except for the Negro; that we have no second-class citizens, except for Negros; that we have no caste system, no ghettos, no master race, except with respect to the Negroes?"

"Now the time has come for this nation to fulfill its promise. The events in Birmingham and elsewhere have so increased the cries for equality that no city or state or legislative body can prudently choose to ignore them."

" The fires of frustration and discord are burning in every city, North and South. . . . We face, therefore, a moral crisis as a country and a people. It cannot be met by repressive police action. It cannot be quieted by token moves or talk. It is a time to act in the Congress, in your state local legislative body, and above all, in all of our daily lives."

"Those who do nothing are inviting shame as well as violence. Those who act boldly are recognizing right as well as reality."

On the day Medgar Evers was buried, President Kennedy sent to Congress a civil rights bill which guaranteed equal accommodation in all segments of public life.

"President Kennedy has stolen my heart. He has done the right thing, as the leader of the nation, by sending the message clearly to the citizens that segregation and discrimination is morally wrong,"

(11-21-1963) the President asked economic advisers to prepare "War on Poverty" program for 1964.

(11-22-1963) President John F. Kennedy was assassinated...

Gravely shocked in deep disappointment, I questioned... *"Just as the passage of the civil rights bill seems closer...the bill will not be signed into law... it seems not by the proposer. Who will be the next in line? It seems like all hope is gone. President Kennedy aided the struggle... had to leave the struggle alone!"*

President John F. Kennedy's "Address to the Nation," in its entirety is based on, the consequences of the development of the slave system in the 1600s, by the devoid of quilt and shame, creating a white society under the influence of a false sense of superiority that falsely justified treating black society as inferior – with inferior opportunity to become financially successful. John F. Kennedy clearly revealed the *"Caste system"* that meant: institutional poverty, within the minority.

Beyond the end of slavery, even by 1963, generational discriminatory practices had not healed from the mentalities of a vast percentage of the American society. And today discriminatory practices have not totally healed... In 1963, President John F. Kennedy said: *"Laws alone cannot make men right!"*

John F. Kennedy's proposal of the Civil Rights Bill and Abraham Lincoln issue of the Emancipation Proclamation, was at different times in history, yet have similar meaning for black Americans of my generation, especially those with slave ancestry. Lincoln, in his time, challenged the aggressive social pathology of the southern establishment of the bondage of slavery; no other President had ever made such a challenge as Lincoln did. Kennedy spoke directly to white America about the moral crisis, the Jim Crow system of injustice, superiority, inferiority, and inequality. He acted upon his words with a civil rights proposal, no other President dared to challenge such a dangerous risk. Regardless of the political ramifications involved in the presidency of Lincoln or Kennedy, in the mind of the slave as parallel to the African American, a president gave hope – the posibility of the freedom of equality.

Histories truth, if not dismissed, but as a catharsis, bringing to consciousness, the connection to today's social environment; affords open expression, about how to move forward to take a moral approach to changing times.

Malcolm X 1925 - 1965

he encouraged black pride and self determination

Malcolm X, a black Muslim spokesman to the Nation of Islam
he focused attention on conditions of black ghettos in America
voicing genuine frustrations, he proposed a revolutionary program
that called for a separate society for black people
to become removed from institutionalized racial policies
removed from the power structured political oppression
The Civil Rights Movement was a committed organization
demonstrating nonviolent demands for justice and equality
perceived the revolutionary vision of Malcolm as a radical threat
Malcolm, a controversial speaker, yet the messages of exaltation
were electrifying to many a black brother and sister
throughout America and listeners were crossing the color line
Malcolm ended his membership with the Nation of Islam
he went on a pilgrimage to Mecca, the Islamic Holy City
among different races and religions, observing brotherhood
he was inspired by the spirit of unity as the power of one God
In the process of organizing the *Black Political Movement*
(2-21-1965) in the prime of his life, before his work was done
Malcolm was assassinated, sadly he left *the people* behind
Malcolm's philosophical message spoke to people of his time
the people of the presence – the future
"To rise above the racial obstacles by self- determination!"

Martin Luther King Jr. 1929 - 1968

the committed moral leader of America

Martin Luther King Jr. was the leader
of the Southern Christian Leadership Conference
a spiritual leader of the Civil Rights Movement
a Nobel Peace Prize Winner in 1964
The battle for equality for black Americans
was making the white supremacist viciously sore
Martin instilled in the civil rights workers
"to achieve the rightful place in American society
spiritual principle of nonviolence, must be the way!"
as violence met Martin and the workers while singing
"We Shall Overcome Someday!"
Protesters on the faithful mission to right the wrong
faced cruelty, jailing, by overwhelming numbers
After protesters were released, from jail
the mission did not end, but courageously carried on
and the minds restrained by the spiritual songs
Martin was jailed several times, his home was bombed
he was despised, stoned, cursed, and spat upon
he wrote letters from jail and read "The Word"
Many a crusader died in the battle for equality
The legacy of a movement for the freedom of another life
opened the door to a Civil Rights Proposal, that
eventually came into effect as the Civil Rights Bill of 1964
(On April-4-1968) Martin Luther King Jr. was assassinated!
Oh how sad! a divinely committed moral leader was gone
for the American Society to search deep within the conscious
to exercise justice and liberty for ALL

I Have a Dream

By Martin Luther King Jr.

On 8-28-1963, the historical, March on Washington… Martin Luther King Jr. delivers his, I Have a Dream Speech, at the Lincoln Memorial, Nations Capital.

"I say to you today even though we face the difficulties of today and tomorrow, I still have a dream. It is a dream that is deeply rooted in the American dream. I have a dream that one day this Nation will rise up, and live out the true meaning of its creed: We hold these truths to be self evident; that all men are created equal."

"I have a dream that one day on the red hills of Georgia the sons of former slaves and the sons of former slave owners will be able to sit down together at the table of brotherhood. I have a dream that one day even the state of Mississippi, a state sweltering with the heat of oppression, will be transformed into an oasis of freedom and justice."

"I have a dream that my four little children one day will live in a nation where they will not be judged by the color of their skin but by the contents of their character."

"I have a dream that one day every valley shall be exalted, every hill and mountain shall be made low. The rough places will be made plain and the crooked places will be made straight. This is the faith that I go back to the South with. With this faith, we will be able to hew out of the mountains of despair the stone of hope. With this faith we will be able to work together, to pray together, to struggle together, to go to jail together, to stand up for freedom together, knowing we will be free one day."

"This will be the day when all of God's children will be able to sing with new meaning, "My country 'tis of thee, sweet land of liberty, of thee I sing. Land where my fathers died, land of the Pilgrim's pride, from every mountain side, let freedom ring."

"And if America is to be a great nation this must become true. So let freedom ring from the prodigious hilltops of New Hampshire; let freedom ring from the mighty mountains of New York. Let freedom ring from the snow-capped Rockies of Colorado. Let freedom ring from the curvaceous peaks of California! Let freedom ring from the heightening Alleghenies of Pennsylvania! But not only that. Let freedom ring from stone mountain of Georgia. Let freedom ring from every hill and molehill of Mississippi, from every mountainside."

"When we allow freedom to ring from every town and every hamlet, from every state and every city, we will be able to speed up that day when all of God's children, black men and white men, Jews and Gentiles,

Protestants and Catholics, will be able to join hands and sing in the words of the old Negro spiritual "Free at last! Free at last! Great God Almighty, we are free at last!"

Coretta Scott King 1927 - 2005

a follower of the dream

She represents natural beauty
spiritual poise and royalty
She knows how to stand by her man
under any kind of pressure
she never lets go of his hand
Her challenge is to continue to redeem
a better and greater American society
she is committed to following the dream
wife of the late Martin Luther King
the beautiful lady is Coretta the Queen

Excerpt from Mrs. Coretta Scott King's speech at the
Memphis City Hall (4-8-1968)

"But then, I ask the question: "How many men must die before we can really have a free and peaceful society?" How long will it take? If we can catch the spirit, and the true meaning of this experience, I believe that this Nation can be transformed into a society of love, of justice, and brotherhood where all men can really be brothers."

Robert Kennedy (1925 – 1968)

the unselfish man

Robert Kennedy, a 1968 leading candidate
for the Democratic Presidential Nomination
his leadership ideology was to end the violence
the disenchantment by the turbulence of the day
to end the division between the poor and the affluent
between age groups and between blacks and whites
To obtain justice for all, Robert would be persuasive
because he believed in America as an unselfish country
Robert would make this his main objective
In (June, 1968) Robert Kennedy was shot and later
on (June 6, 1968) he died. Hopeful supporters had put faith
in him for change, the light of the new dawn was now dim
the ideology for Americans to join the band
with Robert Kennedy himself, *the unselfish man*

Disillusion

written within a period of time after the death of Robert Kennedy in 1968

Revolution?... supposedly construction
yet, only to leave behind this destruction
this contagious corruption… revolution…
the vision for a day with a brand new toy
for playing that once boosted the ego
no longer creates the joy
These changing times of more confusion
where have all the laughter gone?
everyone seem to be going their own way
dealing with their own disillusion…
where is the laughter refusing to subside
the young ones, dancing on the side walk
adding some hope to the stride?
Hope… not meaning continuing turbulence
where is the shoulder to lean on now
to help calm the anxiety…the pain?
where is the laughter through the strain?
perhaps in the wind fleeing too
my brother, my sister, through uncertain days
my Lord…what are we now to do?

Election Day November 2000

A citizen voices the candidate of choice, a constitutional right
I cast a vote, expecting within hours to know the outcome
the close election race, winning could go either way
For Republican George W. Bush and Democrat Al Gore
each needed a majority of the Florida votes
Gore had won Florida, came on the media report
later it was reported that Bush had won Florida
Bush cheered a winning delight, yet later, tension broke out
of certain counties of Florida, Gore demanded a recount
Democratic lawyers for Gore; Republican lawyers for Bush
made a series of court appeals. The Supreme Court deliberated
Gore's recount was overturned, he compiled with the ruling
his concession speech was heartfelt and soothing
he toned down the controversy, well, the rest is history
Legislation for election, I had not taken the time to learn
the voting system I believed in, without a concern
now it seemed like there were some flaws in the system
laws discovered before Election Day can be worked out
to assure the vote of each citizen will definitely count
to keep a fair and simple process for voters everyone
without the Supreme Court judges deciding the outcome
of the candidate I like as one to serve the country right

This is the Day

September 14, 2001, National Day of Prayer and Remembrance, due to the Terrorist Attacks on Tuesday September 11, 2001

(a poetic essay)

The terrorist airplane crash attacks on America were abrupt and mysterious... killing thousands of Americans and wounding many. life in America as we knew it came to a disrupted change by shock, hurt, broken hearts, uncertainty, fear, anger and mourning. The question plagued into consciousness: "Where do we go from here?" The portrayal of unity, tireless heroic rescue efforts, concern and the compassion of ordinary citizens helping wounded human beings mobilized into consciousness, amid the disastrous images.

This is the day to remember to discourage terrorism of any form or fashion in foreign countries, in America and in the world.

This is the day to remember to honor the lost lives and the wounded bodies and souls from the terrorist attacks on America by changing our lives, as individuals of America for the better. Beyond the thick plaguing ash drifting over the atmosphere of New York City, caused by the terrible huge destruction on the World Trade Center, the damage to the Pentagon in Washington DC, the airplane crash sight in rural Pennsylvania, a plane that also had been taken over by terrorists, the answer sustains by the providence of God for individuals of America to turn to, in order to move forward making democracy even stronger. This is the day of prayer and remembrance.

May God Bless America

Message Above the Storm

(a poetic essay)

The providence of the truth of God abides above all things. (8-8-2005) hurricane Katrina ravaged New Orleans! Amid the furious winds and flood waters, people survived and people died.

Thousands of people were jammed packed in the New Orleans Superdome, as hurricane Katrina destroyed overwhelming numbers of homes. Making its mark on New Orleans, and finally moved on....

The desolate went treading through the debris ridden water. Challenging survival each day grew more and more tougher – individuals were grabbing onto things, what ever food product or item insight, helplessly caught up in trouble – in deep desperation, questioning the slow evacuation. "When in need for evacuation – are we poor people any less?..Does the government care about us poor people in this horrific mess?... They are calling us refuges in our own home of America!"

The excuse for the delayed evacuation turned out to be; a process was not in place for such a widespread catastrophe. Four days after Katrina moved on, evacuation finally begun. Because of the heavy flow, a great many of the stranded had to wait. The government hand to offer, had offered a little too late ....

Many a poor family, of good will, use to living quite comfortably, was now forced to another shelter, homeless in another city. Ordinary folk, greatly reached out to evacuees in a time of major need. Will we Americans persist to reach out each day to lives in ruins – or forget and fall back into our own concerns?

Rain falls, and wind blows, on the caring or careless, rich or poor. Lives amid deep destruction, some cannot help but die. To save as many lives as possible, takes the *emergent attempt* to try. The light of God's reality shines clear above the dark catastrophe.

Michael Jackson 1958 - 2009

the greatest entertainer of his time

(a poetic essay)

Michael Jackson was the undisputed, greatest entertainer of his time. As a child performer, he missed out on some of the experiences of childhood, yet was family oriented, but to the world misunderstood. Michael was the lead singer in the group of brothers, *the famous Jackson Five*, Michael would go on to claim great success as a solo artist – creating many songs, dance moves, and videos like no other.

A humanitarian, listed in the *Guinness Book of World Records.* Achieving worldwide fame, Michael was subjective to tabloid frenzy. The sensationalists took every opportunity to slander his name. Michael was unique, yet very willingly shared his expertise. *The King of Pop* himself, could appreciate the talent of someone else.

To all of you sensationalist out there, I say to you: "How can you judge Michael, did you ever walk in his shoes?...did you grow up, as a performer dealing with tabloid news?" You never grew up having to worry about Hollywood appeal, and disappointed by the acne on your face in the adolescence years. Michael had to dodge for cover, and perform before million, to please every body. Some spectators were not his friends, some were against the color of his skin, like he had no right, to hold such a title as *the King of Pop,* after all, he wasn't white. "Were you ever in court accused of something you did not do... defending yourself before a world of millions of eyes on you?"

The pressures of Michael's life circumstance got heavy. Away from it all, he needed to find space, solace and privacy. Loyal fans of Michael loved him, and longed for his come back, missing his great performances, singing and dancing like magic.

Imperfect people themselves have no ability to judge Michael. His Innermost feelings: fears, joys, his laughter, pain and tears. I believe – his love is now at peace, resting in Heaven above.

Eye Witnessing the Vision

(a poetic essay)

(6-3-2008) the evening of the Democratic Convention, Senator Barack Obama accepts the Presidential Nomination, followed by a speech on his walk of life and political plans. Obama, if President, will inherit a growing recession in the land. Mismanagement of Wall Street big bank investors and real estate companies; greed; job lost, and home foreclosures; a lack of health care; the unfair tax breaks for the wealthy; the achievement gap in education, are devastating circumstances. Obama delivers a great message of change from a national view. Many citizens feel the same way too – *a change is well overdue.* The middle class and the working poor are feeling the impact, while billions of dollars are spent on the war in Iraq.

Listening to the *common sense factor* of Obama's brilliant mind, citizens goes from explosive applauding…to spellbind. He gives the appearance of a naturally poised character; his courage always glows… Barack Obama is now the man, the whole world knows. His opponents insist on saying: "Obama is too young and inexperienced." Obama expresses an appealing confidence in his ability to make a difference. It became very apparent, his supporters trusted in his sincerity….

(On 11-4-2008) Barack H. Obama won the Presidential race. The final piece of the puzzle to the historical celebration is now in place….the son, the man, the husband, the father, the friend, Barack H. Obama will become inaugurated as the 44th President of the USA – the seat, he will hold, as the first African American!

Yesterday, Abe said, "A house divided cannot stand!"
Martin said, "We as a people will get to the promised land!"
Obama is a beacon of hope. "Citizen are joining the band!"

A Change has Come to America

(a poetic essay)

(January 20, 2009) People are descending on the Nations Capital, to eye witness the first African American, Barack H. Obama to become sworn in as the 44th President of the United States. They are appearing constantly like a sea of humanity, from different walks of life. Some folk have traveled here from as far away as Africa; no one seems at all bothered by the bitter cold weather. People are waving American flags in the air, and making a euphoric sound: "Yes We Can!" Journalists are chatting with persons of different races. Some are doing a little dance and singing! I am warm at home, watching the amazing events unfold on television. But feeling like I'm missing out on being in Washington, among the people, eye witnessing in person, history being made ...

Only four decades ago, in the (1950s and 60s) Martin Luther King Jr. and many other courageous crusaders for civil rights, paid the ultimate price, placing their lives in harms way – in the battle, to achieve equal opportunity for African Americans..... making this moment happen!...

"Barack H. Obama is sworn in as the, 44th President of the Untied States!" I never knew I would see the day, an African American become the Commander in Chief of this Nation! This day was impossible to imagine for the slaves who built the White House, centuries ago, that a black President and his family would be residing there. This historical milestone assures African Americans that the centuries of struggles, the wounded and deaths for Civil Rights were not in vain.

This inauguration allows me to feel a renewed sense of liberation and inclusion in this land of my birthright ...

The President profoundly believes, "A Change has Come to America!" "I believe that God's guiding light of truth is in the midst of change.

From Katherine Hagans Clark

August 1 2009

To: President Barack H. Obama
The White House
1600 Pennsylvania Ave. NW

Dear Mr. President

I am an African American woman, and grew up in Wilson County, North Carolina in the 1940s. My father was a sharecropper with the help of family members. Living in the town of Wilson in the 1950s, I obtained a high school education in the year of 1955. I am 71 years old, a retired seamstress, the mother of three adult daughters and a son, now residing in Heaven. His life on earth was cut short at the young age of twenty six, like two many of our young men die by the hands of another young man. I have five grandchildren, one of which I have been raising as my own son since the age of six weeks, he's now sixteen. I have four great grandchildren. We are a close knit family.

I have written a collection of expressive poetry that includes spiritually enlightening, historical, and motivational for the best of character. Young people of today could use my poetry, but to appeal to the general public as well. My poetry that is reminiscent of my youthful years in Wilson County on the farm, are writings of a mystical revealing (even to me) of how we as a sharecropping family, upheld the strong will to recognize the creative and spiritual value in survival. That thought brings to mind some of my most favorite lines of poetry.

Abiding Above the Struggle

It is the post Depression era
Folk are adding the laughter and sharing in the sorrow
Neighbors far and near lend a helping hand
The school house is entwining with the family structure
The church house is adding song and dance to living
Instilling faith abiding above the struggle
The congregation is worshipping the Holy Ghost
Elders discipline anybody's children
Some practices in society need never to change

Mr. President, your family as the First Family is ideal. I cannot be more proud of you as President of the United States of America, with the obvious interest of the American people in mind as a whole. May God bless you and all members of your family.

Yours Truly
Katherine Clark *Katherine Clark*

THE WHITE HOUSE

WASHINGTON

November 9, 2009

Dear Friend:

Thank you for your kind note and enclosure. Your thoughtful words join a chorus of millions of Americans who are eager to lead our Nation towards a brighter tomorrow.

Each day, I am inspired by the encouraging messages of hope and determination I have received from people across the country. With the magnitude of challenges we face, we will only overcome them if our imagination is joined to common purpose.

The future we leave to our children and grandchildren will be determined by our willingness to shoulder each other's burdens, take great risks, and move forward as one people and one Nation. With your help, we will build on what we have already achieved and lay a new foundation for real and lasting progress.

Sincerely,